Raising Writers

Raising Writers

Understanding and Nurturing
Young Children's Writing Development

Ruth E. Shagoury

Lewis and Clark College

PEARSON

Boston   New York   San Francisco
Mexico City   Montreal   Toronto   London   Madrid   Munich   Paris
Hong Kong   Singapore   Tokyo   Cape Town   Sydney

Executive Editor: Aurora Martínez Ramos
Editorial Assistant: Kara Kikel
Director of Professional Development: Alison Maloney
Marketing Manager: Danae April
Production Editor: Janet Domingo
Editorial Production Service: DB Publishing Services, Inc.
Composition Buyer: Linda Cox
Manufacturing Buyer: Linda Morris
Design and Electronic Composition: Schneck-DePippo Graphics
Cover Administrator: Kristina Mose-Libon

For related titles and support materials, visit our online catalog at www.pearsonhighered.com.

Between the time website information is gathered and then published, it is not unusual for some sites to have closed. Also, the transcription of URLs can result in typographical errors. The publisher would appreciate notification where these errors occur so that they may be corrected in subsequent editions.

Library of Congress Cataloging-in-Publication Data
Shagoury, Ruth.
   Raising writers : understanding and nurturing young children's writing development / Ruth Shagoury.
     p. cm.
   Includes bibliographical references and index.
   ISBN–13: 978-0-205-51461-8 (alk. paper)
   ISBN–10: 0-205-51461-8 (alk. paper)
   1. English language–Composition and exercises–Study and teaching (Early childhood). 2. Language arts (Early Childhood) 3. Language acquisition. I. Title.
   LB1139.5.L35R35 2009
   372.62 ' 3—dc22   2008002488

10 9 8 7 6

**Allyn & Bacon
is an imprint of**

www.pearsonhighered.com

For
Molly and Jacob

Contents

Acknowledgments

As a way of publicly saying "thanks," I would like to acknowledge the many people who helped me in the research and writing of this book. My first thanks go, of course, to the children who have gracefully tolerated my intrusions and allowed me to learn from them. For over twenty years, I have spent time working with young writers who have been patient with me, as well as willing to share their amazing insights and humor.

I can't begin to express all that I owe to another longtime friend and collaborator: Brenda Power. She not only helped me frame the ideas into a proposal, but read every word, offered advice at each step of the process, and kept me going every time I got discouraged. Her editorial support, suggestions for revisions, and deep knowledge of the field made the book possible. I am grateful to be able to continue to learn from Brenda, always running to catch up with her thoughts that leap ahead of me. Thanks for your endless generosity, Brenda.

I am especially grateful to Andie Cunningham—colleague, co-researcher, teacher, and close friend. She is fearless in her defense of children and respect of their abilities. She never lets me get away with considering anything *cute*. (Andie, I have banned that word from my vocabulary.) I learned so much from her wisdom, risk taking, and keen insights during the four years she welcomed me into her kindergarten classroom. It is a joy to write and teach with her now at the college level. Namaste.

Many teachers allowed me access to their classrooms and their students to continue to collect data, test out ideas, hone theories—and delight in classroom communities. Grateful thanks to: Terra Brackman, Jenny Francis, Melissa Kolb, Kerri Lesh, Elizabeth Parks, and Kelly Petrin.

I am also grateful to my writing group—Kimberly Campbell, Melina Dyer, and Melanie Quinn for their encouragement and support. Their careful reading and inspired questions both stimulated and nudged me forward.

Many thanks to Aurora Martínez Ramos, editor and advisor on this project. I appreciated our conversations whether in person, on the phone, or even in emails from other continents! Thanks for your unfailing confidence and enthusiasm for the project.

Thanks to those who reviewed the manuscript and provided helpful comments: Carla Chavez, Kathryn A. Egawa, Wendy A. Ellis, Marsha Jane Jackson, Richard P. Santeusanio, Lauren M. Santeusanio, and Emily Tischer.

John and June Rogers continue to support my work through their generous contributions and commitment in the Mary Stuart Rogers Foundation. Many thanks!

Jim Whitney's genius with photography is an incredible gift to me and the many educators he helps by bringing our work alive visually. His keen eye and perfectionism allow readers to see the environments that nurture young writers. How did I get so lucky to be able to share my research and writing with the love of my life? Your support made this book possible.

Raising Writers

Paying Attention to Miracles

L anguage opens up the world of communication, creating and expanding the potential for sharing our wishes, thoughts, and needs. We can talk about a remembered past and an imagined future through the wonder of a string of words.

There is a magic and mystery to the acquisition and development of human language. In the last ten years, the field of language development has been revolutionized by intriguing new studies that show the astounding capabilities of newborns' minds, rich with language-learning resources. We now know more about the evolution of infants' speech sounds to toddlers' mastery of complex grammar to the continued refinement of vocabulary and academic language of children in school. Early childhood specialists have come to understand the sophisticated oral language forms that very young children use, and the developmental continuum that can be mapped out to help teachers both appreciate what children are currently able to do—and recognize what is likely to follow developmentally.

There has been a less-publicized body of research that also has the power to revolutionize the field of language development: the equally astounding capabilities of young children in literate cultures to apply their language-learning resources to the written word.

Abilities like those of five-year-old Carrie, a young neighbor of mine: One afternoon, I was having a coffee break with my good friend—and fellow busy mother—Laurie. Our older children were still in school, and this was an anticipated time together to chat and sip coffee. I knew Carrie was upstairs; we couldn't miss her presence: she stomped and slammed doors, and we could hear her loud muttering and complaining.

"I told her she needed to pick up her room if she wanted to come and join us," Laurie explained.

Suddenly the noise stopped and a piece of paper floated down the stairway.

Laurie scooped up the paper and we both laughed as we deciphered the following message: "Mom, I don't want to pick up my room" (Figure 1.1).

"Well, young lady, I'm sorry you don't want to, but you have to pick up your room!" Laurie called back up the stairs.

FIGURE 1.1

Carrie's Note:
"I don't want to pick up my room."

Silence . . . followed by another paper floating toward us. (See Figure 1.2.) "I can't pick up my room. I can't. I can't."

How did Carrie know how to use the written word to communicate with us when her stomping and sighing failed? What allowed her to translate sounds to written symbols when she had not yet been to school or been "taught" to read or write? Carrie was already on the road to literacy, using her language skills to communicate with the written word just as she has acquired her spoken language prowess.

Like oral language, written language follows a recognizable developmental path. Though boundaries around stages are wide, it helps educators who work with young children to understand what to expect in terms of literacy development. Educators must also understand the "messiness" of real-

FIGURE 1.2

Carrie's Note:
"I can't pick up my room. I can't. I can't."

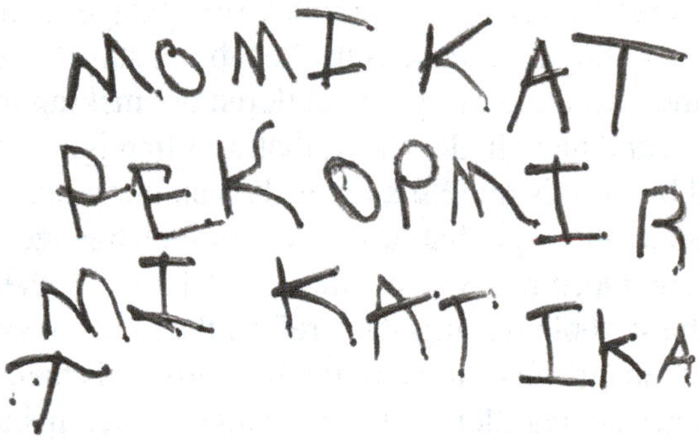

MOMI KAT
PEK OPMIR
MI KAT IKA

world learning, always situating what children say—and write—within a context. The theoretical grounding of this contextualized developmental lens comes from the work of Jerome Harste (1984) and, more recently, Anne Haas Dyson (2003). Dyson reminds us that it is crucial to "articulate a developmental vision that moves beyond the textually tidy developmental path" (p. 7) and embrace the complex sources and inventions from which children draw.

This book does offer a "developmental" perspective, one that represents a view of children changing over time; seen through a sociolinguistic lens, "development is a process . . . not a series of sequentially learned skills" (Dyson, 2003, p. 11; see also Miller & Goodnow, 1995; Rogoff, 1990; Watson-Gegeo, 1992).

Teachers who respect children's astounding capabilities and have the opportunity to see the patterns that emerge from an analysis of children's language in context can listen to their students and look at their written work with a new and appreciative lens.

A Continuum for Language Development

Where Does It Start?

Babies have fun making noises. They experiment with the range of sounds they can produce, from coos and gurgles to snorts, blowing bubbles, and loud "raspberries." This kind of playful vocalization happens when babies are by themselves and when they interact with adults. As their babbling becomes more advanced, they use the sounds of the adult language that surrounds them, with the rhythms and intonations of the native language they are already beginning to acquire. Babies at this stage of language development sound as though they are really talking, even ending their "sentences" with pauses, and sounding conversational, though their babbles make no sense.

Babbling is more than just "play" for babies (Galinkoff & Hirsh-Pasek, 2000). They must practice the sounds of their language in order to produce real words. Even deaf babies of deaf parents, whose first language is sign, "babble" with their hands, making gestures that mimic sign language but are not actual signs and do not convey meaning (Petito & Marentette, 1991).

Young children in literate cultures go through a scribble-writing stage as they acquire written language. Scribble writing in a sense is the "babbling stage" for literacy. We are so familiar with the scribble writing that children do, making marks on the page in a seemingly random and meaningless way, that we often ignore the importance of this stage. Like babbling, it is more than play. It is an important stage where young children make marks on the page that look like written language, though these marks do not yet represent any meaning. As we will see in Chapter 2, the markings children make during the scribble writing stage reflect the kinds of symbol systems that are used in the written language of the culture that surrounds them.

The babbling and scribble stages are parallel tracks on a language acquisition continuum. In the pages that follow, I will frame a lens for viewing children's oral and written language along a developmental continuum. (See Table 1.1.) The chapters of this book will examine the categories, with numerous examples from young children as well as strategies for understanding and nurturing written language at all stages of development. Table 1.1 lists the major theorists whose research forms the basis for the written language development continuum, which is the focus of this book.

The five basic categories along the continuum are ones that teachers and care-givers can easily recognize in the children they encounter. Recognizing what a child can do today helps us know what to be watching for and suggesting as "next steps" on the road to literacy.

Early Communication

After babbling and scribble writing, the "next big step" in language development on these parallel tracks deals with categories and representation. In oral language, babies begin to use everything at their disposal to communicate their needs and desires. This can be in the form of grunts and sounds, shaking the head, and especially pointing and eye gaze. These signals are important because they herald the beginning of babies' ability to intentionally communicate. Though these babies are still pre-verbal, they are creating perfect opportunities for language learning. "These episodes are 'hot spots' for vocabulary learning. . . . Since mothers often put their babies' intentions into words (Oh, it's the *cheese* you want!), babies are hearing words for precisely what they are focused on at the moment" (Golinkoff & Hirsh-Pasek, 2000, p. 71).

Through their continued exposure to the sound patterns they are hearing in these language learning contexts, babies begin to recognize patterns and find words in the language streams swirling around them. Once they put meaning into these units they recognize, they are more than simply patterns, but true words. Now babies recognize these words, but are still grappling with how to actually produce them. At this stage, it is absolutely essential that parents and caregivers honor the communication attempts of their babies. Numerous studies show that parental responsiveness to babies' communicative efforts contribute to language growth (Bruner 1983; Sachs, Bard, & Johnson, 1981; Schiefflin & Ochs, 1983).

Just as babies acquiring oral language show a recognizable stage where they are becoming active communicators, young children acquiring written language show

TABLE 1.1 Continuum for Language Development

Normal Oral Development	The Babbling Period	Pointing and One-word Categorizing	First Words and Growing Vocabulary	Simple Sentences	Grammatical Capability
	• Produces vocalizations that sound like language • Practices sounds and intonations reflective of the language of the adults in the environment	• Begins to use communication devices (vocalizes and points) • Attributes meaning to words or concepts • Produces single words to represent a word or concept	• Uses social words and naming words • Able to form categories and use fast-mapping	• Power of two-word utterances to represent complex thought • Telegraphic speech • Relies on context to communicate • Understands and uses syntax	• Understands sentence structure • Uses language to accomplish goals • Social conventions • Playfulness in language
Normal Written Development	Scribble Writing	Beginning Representation	Sound-Symbol Relationship	Beginning Narrative	Using Writing to Get Things Done
	• Produces marks on a page that look like written language • Practices the markings that reflect the written language of the culture	• Uses the page as a communication device • Produces first symbols on paper to represent meaning	• Creates words on the page using letters to represent sounds • Uses different social forms of writing	• Understands and uses sequence • Represents complex thought on the page • Relies on context to communicate	• Uses writing conventions • Uses genre conventions • Playfulness in writing • Uses writing to accomplish social and academic goals
Research Base	Anne Haas Dyson Harste, Woodward, & Burke	Donald Graves Harste, Woodward, & Burke Anne Haas Dyson Glenda Bissex Ruth Hubbard Susan Bridge	Donald Graves Lucy Calkins Glenda Bissex Ruth Hubbard/ Shagoury Carol Chomsky Sandra Wilde	Arthur Applebee Anne Haas Dyson Gordon Wells Judy Hilliker Shirley Brice Heath	Lucy Calkins Katie Wood Ray Anne Haas Dyson Emilia Ferreiro & Ana Teberosky Sandra Wilde

parallel—and equally important—growth. In the *beginning representation* stage, they are beginning to use the page as a communication device. Young children at this stage are moving beyond scribble writing and producing symbols on paper to represent meaning.

Five-year-old Song gives a gentle tug to my sleeve and passes me a sheet of paper (see Figure 1.3). "What does this say?" she asks.

I look at the string of letters: *Mtiokyeiko*. Under it is a picture of a house and the circled word *NO*.

"Hmm, what do you think it says?"

Song takes the paper back in one hand and runs her finger under the letters at the top of the page. Slowly, she "reads," "I-Want-Ruth."

I smile and ask, "And this?"

"It says, 'No.'"

"And tell me about your drawing," I ask, expecting her to tell me it's her house. "A dog," she tells me.

The surprise registers on my face. "A dog?"

Now it's her turn to smile. "A dog is inside the house."

Song is clearly a writer in transition. She knows that letters mean something; someone who knows how to read can get their meaning. Song writes a string of letters and assumes there is an inherent meaning, so she asks me to tell her what it says. But when I turn it back to her, she "reads" a message. And on the same page, she has written a word that others could read as well: *NO*.

Just as it is absolutely essential that parents and caregivers honor the communication attempts of their babies, it is vital that caregivers and educators honor these early written attempts. It is still language that we are nurturing, though it is in written rather than oral form. Our responsiveness to young children's written communicative efforts stimulate interest and show children they have agency through their print.

Using Symbol Systems

What an exciting moment when we hear a baby utter her first word! Parents document these moments, delighted that

FIGURE 1.3
Song's doghouse

their children are beginning to share what they're thinking. This is a natural part of human development that occurs in every language around the world; still, we celebrate it as a miracle. While we recognize its importance as a milestone, most adults don't realize the complexity and difficulty of this task of learning words. Those of us who struggle to learn a second language get a glimpse of the difficult task that a baby goes through every day, when we try to recognize a word in a string of speech in our new language or wrestle to retrieve a word we thought we knew.

The ability to understand words exceeds the ability to produce them. In order to continue to grow vocabularies and complex word meaning, children experiment with their words in different contexts. They use labeling words to build categories such as "animals" or "food" and social words, such as "bye-bye" and "hi." And they rely on their parents and caregivers to respond to their attempts using language that builds from these tries, rather than directs them.

In this stage, babies show that they are able to apply a new label from a single exposure. This behavior is called *fast-mapping,* and is a key to continued language learning success. It is also a sign that children have entered a period sometimes called the "vocabulary growth spurt." Toddlers at this stage are learning unfamiliar words by the process of elimination.

For example, imagine a busy mother making supper while her nineteen-month-old son Mark plays with four kitchen "toys" his mom has dumped on the floor to entertain him. Mark knows the words for "pot," "spoon," and "cup." But there is a new utensil, one he's never played with before or heard its name: a garlic press.

"Oh, honey, I need the garlic press," Mom tells him and walks toward Mark to pick it up. Mark looks at his mom, looks at his "toys" and grabs the garlic press and passes it to her. Mark is fast-mapping: *The new name I'm hearing must map to the one I don't already have a name for.* Toddlers like Mark who assume (just as adults do) that new names go to a category without a name can learn new vocabulary items very quickly.

The key role of the adults is to provide abundant and context-rich language. Numerous studies show that a child's vocabulary can be predicted from the number of words a child hears (Hart & Risley, 1995).

In writing, children also experience an incredible parallel leap in their development. They show they have the ability to create symbols in the form of words on the page, making the developmental jump to writing using recognizable cultural symbols of literacy.

Picture five-year-old Molly, a writer in the midst of this transition. Under her drawing of flowers, she has written: *FRVSH.* (See Figure 1.4 on page 8.)

"Can you read me what you wrote today, Molly?" I ask.

"Flowers. Vase. And my hand."

"Wow! That's amazing writing! I can read that, too. Can I make a copy?"

"Sure, but I'm not done."

She quickly writes another sequence of letters: *mihiN mm.*

"What does that say?" I ask.

"Can you read it? I don't even know what it is when I wrote."

Molly is in that phase where she is beginning to put the sounds she hears down on paper. It's more a label than a story, but it shows she knows she can write things that she can read back. But she also hangs on to the belief, like Song in the earlier example, that the letters themselves magically mean something that a reader will know and can tell her—even if she is the writer!

Both young writers are at an important stage in their writing development. I see them turning the corner in their ability to make meaning on the page—and read back the words they write.

Jacob, on the other hand, shows me that he has turned that corner. When I ask him to show me his writing during writing workshop time in his kindergarten class, he points to a journal page with brilliant colors, a large mountain-like shape, and the letters *C A N*. (See Figure 1.5.)

"Oh, you're writing another story about volcanoes? Can you read it to me?"

"Sure. The volcano is shooting fire on the sand. See? Sand," he reads, pointing to the letters *CAN*.

"And the water's goin' back in," he explains.

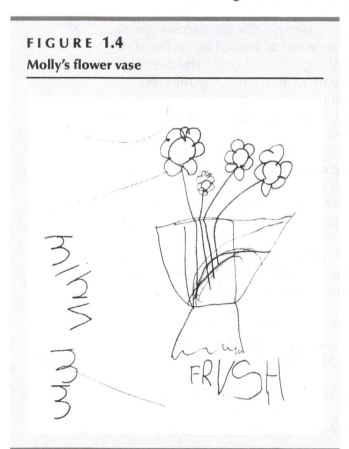

FIGURE 1.4

Molly's flower vase

"Anything else you want to add?"

"I'll write volcano, I think." He takes his crayon in hand, *V, V* . . ." and slowly says the whole word "volcano." "*Q, O.* Volcano!"

"You wrote a lot! Do you hear any more sounds?"

We both say "volcano" slowly and Jacob adds *QNO*.

Jacob can write and read back what he has written. In a sense, he has cracked the code, not relying on the magic of someone who can "read" to tell him what his letters say. He can do it himself.

Just like fast-mapping, the ability to "invent spellings" heralds the beginning of a written vocabulary growth spurt. Young children who can represent the sounds they hear by writing some letters can use whatever letter-sound combinations they have at their disposal and apply them to new situations. With more practice and exposure, their written words grow toward conventional spelling and are easier for others around them to decode.

Remember Carrie, whose frustration at cleaning her room was so eloquently expressed in her notes to her mother? She shows that she has discovered this powerful tool and knows how to use it to affect the world around her. About a year after the "room-cleaning notes" episode, when Carrie was about five and a half years old, I moved to a town a few miles away. One day I called to chat with Laurie, and Carrie answered the phone.

"Can you tell your mom to call me?" I asked.

A few minutes later, my phone rang and it was Laurie.

"Did you want me to call you?" she asked.

"Yes. Did Carrie tell you?"

Pause. "I think so. She left me a note." (See Figure 1.6, "colrufe.")

We could both decipher her message to "call Ruthie [rufie]." This is more than a cute example of a bright child writing notes. Carrie shows that she understands the ways she can use symbolic representation to "tell" someone something. It shows her ability to use different forms of writing, from notes to express her feelings to relaying information. The more she writes, the more her written vocabulary will grow.

FIGURE 1.5
Jacob's volcano story

FIGURE 1.6
Carrie's note:
"Call Ruthie"

Simple Sentences and Beginning Narrative

The ability to put words together to express more complex thoughts is a giant step in both oral and written language production. When babies begin to use two-word utterances, they have much more expressive power. But their words still need some guesswork to discover their meaning. For example, "Daddy hat!" might mean: "That's Daddy's hat," or "Daddy, I want that hat," or "Is Daddy leaving? 'Cause he's putting on his hat." We need to use the context in order to understand what this baby is trying to express. We make interpretations based on the situation, the intonation, and our knowledge of the child.

Babies at this stage show the growing complexity of their thinking; they are exploring relationships and are beginning to share ideas with others. This in turn encourages them to want to learn more. According to Dr. Lois Bloom, "children are motivated to learn more language when their ideas exceed what they are capable of talking about" (Bloom, 1993, p. 47). Parents help their toddlers' speech grow when they assume that their children are expressing meaningful ideas and work to make interpretations, expanding on their words rather than correcting.

Beginning narrative in children's writing also shows the power of more complex and capable thought on the page. Writers at this stage move beyond labeling to telling "stories" of an event.

Cory looked downcast, but was eager to share his writing with me. "Me and Garrett were at school and he said, 'You have a big fat head.' And I felt bad."

"Is that what you wrote about?" I asked. "Can you read it to me?"

"'Big Fat Head,' it says there," he explained, pointing to the letters 'bEGGfat.'"

"Then, I see another guy. 'Big fat head to you!'" (See Figure 1.7.)

Cory is moving beyond labeling to recording more complex events—to telling the story of what happened to him.

Like Cory, Lacey uses her writing as a kind of conversation starter to tell her story. (See Figure 1.8.)

"I went to the Crab Shack with my family for supper," she told me.

FIGURE 1.7

Cory's "Big Fat Head" story

"And I wrote about it in my journal, see? There was seashells and funny skeletons that were like disco skeletons hanging from the ceiling. And there was boats with pop cans. We had fun and I want to go back."

Moving into this stage allows children to express relationships among events and ideas in their written communication. It would be easy to underestimate the tasks that Cory or Lacey are grappling with, or the meaning of their writing without their words of explanation. The importance of "rich interpretation" with children's written work remains crucial.

FIGURE 1.8

Lacey's "Crab Shack" story

Structure and Conventions: Using Language and Writing to Get Things Done

Young children between the ages of two and three are growing in their ability to be fluent and sophisticated language users. Because they now understand the structure of sentences, they move beyond telegraphic speech to the endless variations that word order and word parts allow speakers. They use endings like -*ing,* use plurals markers; they show they are discovering the invisible rules of their language. In fact, it is at this time that children "insist" on the rules, overgeneralizing to make irregular plurals and verbs regular! You may hear a child use words such as "mouses" or "foots," or verbs such as "goed" showing that they have internalized certain patterns in the language they heard and are using.

Children are also learning to ask questions using specific words such as "What?" "How?" and "Why?" These questioning words help children initiate conversations on their own terms, and because the responses will be longer, they also get to hear a lot more language to continue their grammatical spurts.

To be able to accomplish what they desire, children need to acquire specific social conventions. Learning "politeness" terms such as "please" and "thank you" help them become successful in the culture of which they are a part. There are right and wrong ways to ask for things in each culture, and children can only learn these by applying their language skills to situations.

Sometimes those skills are around verbal play and pretending. Telling funny stories and making word plays also show a child's growing grammatical and language sophistication.

Young writers are also learning the "social conventions" of the written word. They may begin by inventing conventions to make their written work easier to read back. For example, look at the device six-year-old Chris employs to separate his words. (See Figure 1.9: "The rabbit is jumpin' on the bricks," with dashes between words.) The convention in written English (and many other languages) is a blank space to separate words. Here, Chris uses a temporary marker he has invented as he progresses toward the conventions of written English. Young writers show they

FIGURE 1.9

Chris uses dashes to separate words.

have entered this next phase in their development when they play with exclamation marks, apostrophes, and other written language conventions.

Another mark of this stage is the use of "story language" typical of the storytelling of their culture. Children write terms as one word such as "*wunsuponatim*" (once upon a time) or finalize their stories with "The End" in imitation of the ways that storytellers communicate with their audiences. Children are using the social "politeness" conventions that their readers will expect.

Response to Young Writers

You can become blind by seeing each day as a similar one. . . . Each day brings a miracle of its own. It's just a matter of paying attention.

—Paul Coelho

Viewing children through a new lens in their oral and written language is an invitation to pay attention to the miracle of each child's abilities. Research in the field suggests a stance that is invitational, nurturing, and, above all, respectful. Whether working with babies' oral language development, or young children's written language, it is crucial to respect young children's communication attempts, provide an environment rich in language, and be prepared to be awed by babies' and young children's capabilities.

When I work with young writers, I ask myself a series of questions:

1. What is the history of this child and this piece of writing?
2. What does this child show that she knows:
   a. About the world?
   b. About language?
3. What is his intent in this piece of writing?
4. How can I help her make her meaning clearer?

Approaching children's writing with these questions may mean learning to listen to children in new ways, not with the intent of correction, but of providing the right kind of support. This support may take a variety of forms, from providing examples, modeling, extended listening, or a nudge to take a risk and learn a new skill.

Deep listening and paying attention to children's literacy helps illuminate those everyday miracles that Coelho invites us to celebrate. They are there waiting for us on the page in the magic of young children's writing.

Three key tenets in language acquisition and development, both oral and written, are:

1. Respect young children's communication attempts.
2. Provide an environment rich in language.
3. Be prepared to be awed by babies' and young children's capabilities.

Those Aren't Just Scribbles
Analyzing Early Writing Attempts

Three-year-old Benton hunches over a piece of discarded typewriter paper, crayon clutched in his chubby fist. The green crayon marks swirl across the page making a seemingly random scribble. (See Figure 2.1.)

"Mommy!" he calls with urgency in his voice.

"What is it, Benton?"

Benton looks at his green crayon marks and "reads" from his paper: "Benton wants to go upstairs right now and Mommy don't like the idea."

Even at his young age, Benton is a writer. Once we as adults begin to understand the links between oral and written language, we can view their earliest attempts at putting crayon or pen on the page in new ways. We can begin to look at the intention behind their communication and the understanding of literacy that these attempts demonstrate. Benton is a member of a literate culture; he sees his parents and the power of the marks they put on paper. In fact, when Benton's mother

Brynna asked him, "Benton, why did you write Mommy a note?" he reminded her of an event from earlier in the day.

"You said Dad, you write a note. And now *I* did it!" Benton's page of scribbles could be discounted as meaningless without an understanding of the context, and without Benton's own report of what his writing means. Those two aspects of writing—context and children's intent—are crucial elements in understanding any piece of writing or drawing.

Current theory in literacy stresses the importance of taking process into account; written language literacy involves "the saga of learning how to mean" (Graves, 2002). Children become aware of the writing demands of each situation, ways that they differ and ways they are alike. It is only through a study of this process, learning from children themselves, that we can come to understand the ways that young children test the boundaries of written language, taking risks and actively using all they know about writing, just as they have done as they have acquired oral language.

FIGURE 2.1

Benton's scribble writing

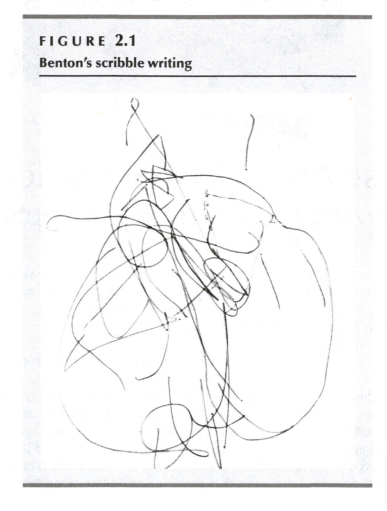

Young children are written language users and learners long before their writing looks representational.

—Harste, Woodward, & Burke

When young children like Benton make their marks on the page, adults usually interpret them as "just scribbles" or "playing around on paper." But just as the babble stage of speaking provides important and intentional practice with the language, based on the intonations of the culture surrounding the speaker, so, too, does "scribble writing" play an important role in the evolution of written language. Children's earliest marks on the page are not random; rather, they are intentional attempts at making meaning with writing.

Leah writes in unconventional script using wavy lines (see Figure 2.2). If we focus on her writing as "product," and notice what she *doesn't* know, it is easy to dismiss all that she *does* know about written language. And Leah knows a great deal: she writes from left to right, across the page, starting at the top and ending at the right-hand lower corner. Her wavy script is similar to the cursive writing she sees her sisters and her parents use. If asked what her writing says, Leah will graciously read it, as she did this piece about her family's new kitten.

FIGURE 2.2

Leah's unconventional script

Four-year-old Fouad also wrote rows of letters. His writing looks more Arabic than English, but like Leah's writing, it is not in conventional script (see Figure 2.3). Fouad does not yet speak enough English to "read" this piece to me or his teacher, but will often "read" his writing in Arabic to his peers and parents.

Cecilia uses a combination of individual, yet often unconventional letters as well as cursive scribble writing in her story about her mother, "Mi Mami en casa" (see Figure 2.4). As young children have more experiences with the print in their environment, and more practice holding writing implements, they begin to create elements of script that adults around them recognize. In this story, Cecilia shows she has the fine motor control to make the individual letter shapes, using *r*'s, *u*'s, and *v*'s as well as wavy script lines. She also demonstrates her understanding of the difference between writing and drawing. Her text is illustrated with a picture of her smiling Mami.

Most often, children will begin using the letters of their name; after all, children see these letters more often and caregivers are likely to write, read, and engage in conversation about them.

FIGURE 2.3
Fouad's unconventional script

FIGURE 2.4
Cecilia's unconventional script

Name:_____ date:_____

My young friend Carrie, age four and a half, drew the following picture of me (see Figure 2.5). When she finished, she wrote several letters at the top of the page: C I O L X. When I asked her to read her story to me, she shook her head, "I don't know how to read—you read it." This is an amazing milestone in young children's writing. Children like Carrie are beginning to write down the letters they know, often from their own name or letters they see around them, as placeholders for meaning. They know that these magic marks can be read by others, and they infer that someone who can read will know what the writing says! When I asked Carrie to tell me what she was thinking when she wrote the letters, she once again demonstrated her literacy understanding. "I was thinking, 'This is Ruth holding lettuce on a stick and she's happy.'" Carrie's writing was intentional; she used the few conventional letters at her disposal to label her drawing. (It was also, I hasten to point out, fictional!)

Chris has many letters in his writing repertoire and uses them to write long stories that he reads back to his audience (see Figure 2.6). Each time he reads them back, he reads the same text, with minor variations: "Chris was walkin' by the river. He fell right into the river. It was cold." His "reading voice" sounds a bit more formal than his conversational voice. It's clear he is able to use the symbols of his culture to represent his story.

Five-year-old Bao Jun's native first language is Cantonese. In September, when I am just learning what all the children in her kindergarten class are "experts" at, Bao Jun tells me she is an "expert at writing in Chinese." She writes pages of Chinese characters to represent her stories, much as Chris has done. Bao Jun's first writing is based on a nonalphabetic language (see Figure 2.7). As she is learning the shapes of a limited number of letters for writing in English, she is also exposed to—and experimenting with—hundreds of complex pictographic-ideographic symbols. Rather than being too complicated a task for her, there is a decided advantage for Bao Jun and other second language learners to keep their first oral and

FIGURE 2.5

Carrie's string of letters

FIGURE 2.6

Chris' string of letters

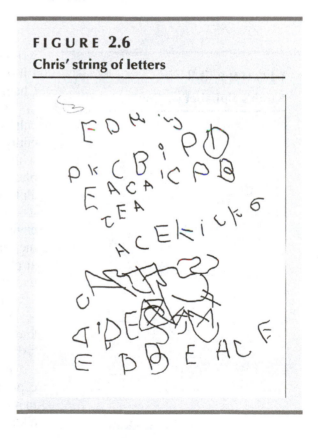

FIGURE 2.7

Bao Jun's Chinese writing

FIGURE 2.8

Sarah's alphabet writing

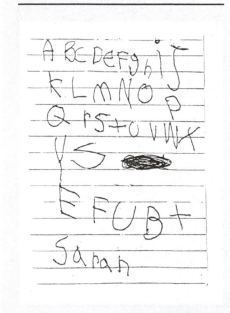

written languages strong as they learn English. I'll return to this discussion in more depth in Chapter 6.

Because it is such a visible aspect of our literate culture here in the United States, "the alphabet" as an entity is often something young children practice, even without instructions to do so. I have numerous examples, in and out of school, of young children writing the alphabet in the order they have learned to sing or recite it—or simply copying a set of symbols they see in the environment, on walls or desks. When asked to "write me something" as we sat next to each other on a long airplane ride, my young seatmate Sarah wrote the letters of the alphabet (see Figure 2.8).

"Tell me about your writing," I asked.

She looked up at me as if I surely should know, then wrote a "label" for her writing: *EFUBT.* "Alphabet," she explained.

Isn't that amazing? Sarah already knows the concept of the alphabet, not just random letters on a page to represent meaning. She also uses the alphabet as a kind of construction kit for putting together a word

(EFUBT = alphabet). (For a thoughtful discussion of the advantages of an alphabetic system, as well as a critique of overemphasis on the alphabetic principles in literacy instruction, see Frank Smith, 2003.)

"As It Happens"

Many children want to depict movement on the page "as it happens" (Hubbard, 1989). Various researchers who have studied preschool children note the importance of motor activity over content, or even color, on the paper (Gibson, 1966). But it is more than the actual arm movement across the page that is important to these young children. In an interesting experiment, Gibson and Yonas (1968) replaced children's markers with ones that didn't leave any traces. Even children below two years of age lost interest in the scribbling if it left no marks. Gibson and Yonas conclude that not only are children interested in the physical action of scribbling, they are very interested in the traces—that record of their motor activity they have left on the page.

In a year-long ethnography looking at young children's writing and drawing, I documented that the actual activity the children are immersed in—scribbling or acting out an event on the page—is partly action and play in the midst of their composing (Hubbard, 1989). (Note: This book was published using my former name of Ruth Hubbard.) I also discovered it serves the important purpose of symbolizing that action on the page itself:

FIGURE 2.9

Ming's action story

> Kelly, for example, was intrigued with a story about an oil tank exploding that she saw on television. My first impression of her from across the room was that she was just fooling around and scribbling this morning, but I was wrong.
>
> "Look at this gas exploding!" Kelly demanded, as she pushed her writing booklet toward me. Her "scribbles" were a way for her to act out the motion she was trying to understand from the explosion she saw on the news, but when she explained it to me, it had become an actual symbol of that action. (Hubbard, 1989, p. 101)

Ming's page of writing details an entire story, but looks like a playful scribble of lines and circles (see Figure 2.9). Without a look at his process and a description from Ming of his story, it would be easy to underestimate the written work Daniel is creating "as it happens."

"See, there's a king up here, and he's up in his castle. But he's got these ene-mies, and there's these soldiers . . ." Ming's fingers follow the action on his page as he tells me his movement-filled adventure.

While Nathan's story seems a bit more representational, it is again the move-ment, and the marks on the page that depict the motion, that are the key to his story. (See Figure 2.10.) Like Ming, Nathan acted out the story on the page with sweeping hand movements as he spoke.

"That's Yoda jumping. And look, that's Darth Mall from Star Wars. Look, Yoda jumps, and look what happens! He jumps and hits the light saber!"

My nod of interest shows Nathan he has an audience, and he launches into the next episode of the saga, pointing to the bottom of the page:

FIGURE 2.10

Nathan's Yoda story

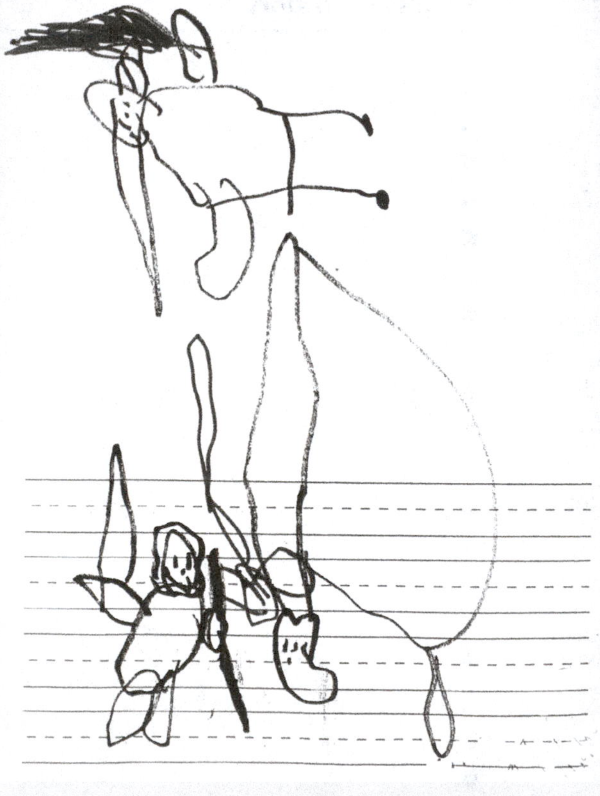

"And look, there's Yoda. He's dead. Yup. He made a choice to jump. He raised his hand by hisself, and his laser . . ." A shrug and upturned hands show that's the end of Yoda.

Nathan was pleased with the action in the story he wrote, even choosing to tell and retell it to children nearby the next day when he took out his writing journal. Once again, he pointed out the path that Yoda took on his ill-fated leap onto his laser. Nathan was successfully reading back the traces he had left to tell his story as he made his mark with crayon on paper.

Beginning Representation

It is clear from these samples that even very young children use the page as a communication device. They make marks that mimic the written symbols of their culture; they create traces to show the movement and action of the stories or information they wish to remember and share. And as they have more experiences with the print that they see and attempt to "read," they want others around them to understand their writing.

Tomas' piece is a fascinating example of a child who is just on the cusp of an important transition to more conventional written words. Big, looping curlicues stream across the page. (See Figure 2.11.) Florence, his kindergarten teacher, pulls up a chair alongside his desk and asks, "What are you writing about today, Tomas?"

His fingers trace the squiggles as he explains, "The kites—the kites are flying." His page represents the movement the kites made as the wind carried them across the sky.

But Tomas is not done with his writing today.

"The kites are flying," Florence says slowly. "Do you want to add anything?"

Slowly, Tomas repeats the same words, then adds: *K, T, R, F.* "The kites are flying," he reads.

KTRF shows the letter name strategy that Tomas shares with other young children who invent their own spellings and use letters to stand for letter names, rather than, as conventionally in spelling, just sounds (Read, 1971).

Deanna's writing, though very different from Tomas', shows a writer at a similar stage in using the page to make meaning. Her mother, literacy researcher Brenda Power, shared the following "language story and literacy lesson" with me when Deanna was six years old.

FIGURE 2.11

Tomas' story:
The kites are flying.

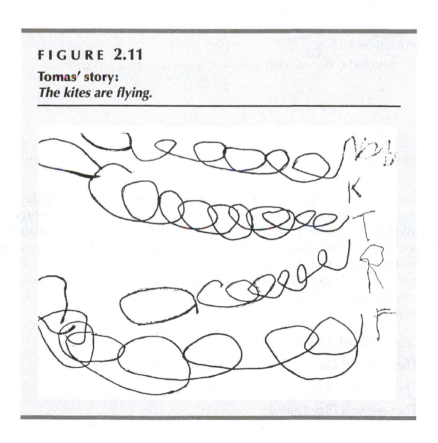

FIGURE 2.12

Deanna's time sheet

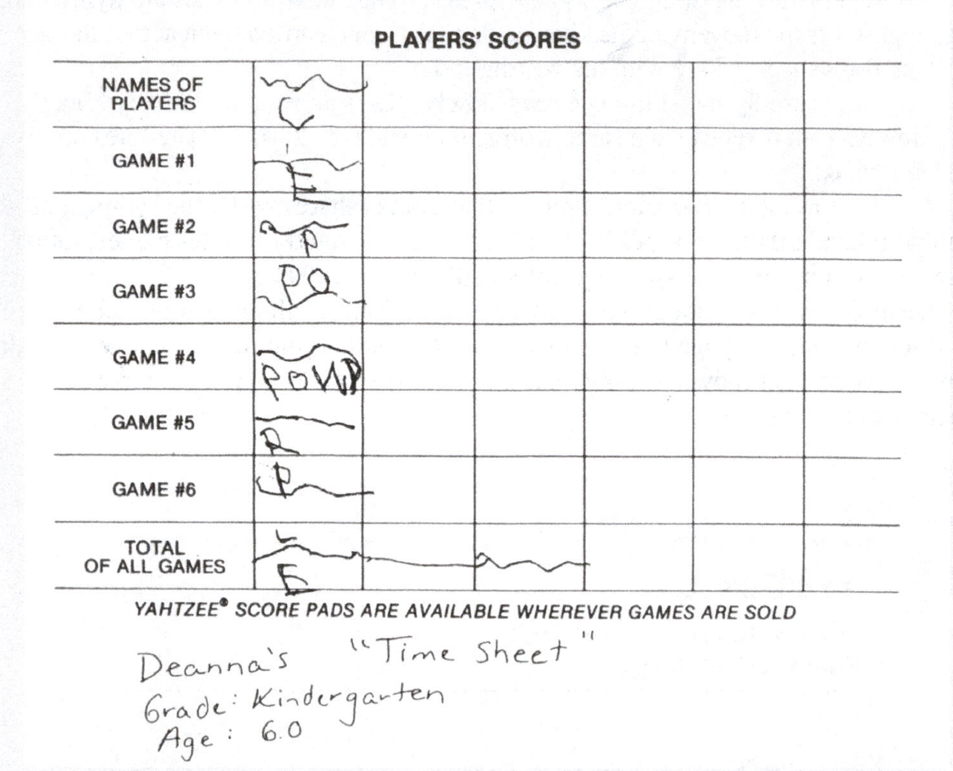

PLAYERS' SCORES

NAMES OF PLAYERS						
GAME #1						
GAME #2						
GAME #3						
GAME #4						
GAME #5						
GAME #6						
TOTAL OF ALL GAMES						

YAHTZEE® SCORE PADS ARE AVAILABLE WHEREVER GAMES ARE SOLD

Deanna's "Time Sheet"
Grade: Kindergarten
Age: 6.0

Deanna and Forrest [her four-year-old neighbor] were playing yesterday afternoon and she was very naughty. So, after he left, I sent her to her room and told her she couldn't come out until she had a plan for tomorrow and she could tell me how they could play together without fighting and getting into so much trouble. I thought she'd come out and tell me something, but she came out and gave me this piece of paper, the back of a Yahtzee score card, which she says is her "Time Sheet" for tomorrow. (See Figure 2.12.) She read it:

"First, we will Color.

Then we will Eat.

Then we will Play.

Then we will Play Outside.

25

Caretakers'
and
Educators'
Role in Young
Children's
Earliest
Writing

Then we will Play Outside with Daddy.

Then we will Read.

Then we will Play some more.

Then we will Eat, then Forest will Leave after we play as much as you
let us."

I asked her what the squiggly lines meant and she said, "Those are all the
letters I could write if I wanted to, but I DON'T." Notice that "play as long
as you let us" at the end has the longest line. (Power, personal communication, 1999)

Deanna is using initial consonants and letters' names to invent spelling, con-
veying her plan for playing without getting into trouble. There is much more she
could write, she lets her mother know, "if she wanted to" but since she doesn't, she
chooses to represent those words with symbolic cursive squiggles.

Just like the earlier examples, without an understanding of the context in which
the writing occurred as well as the young author's intent, the brilliance of the written solution would go unnoticed.

Caretakers' and Educators' Role in Young Children's Earliest Writing

In a fascinating study by researchers Silvia Bell and Mary Ainsworth (1972), infants
were followed for their first year of life to evaluate the impact of response to crying.
Bell and Ainsworth's findings were clear and have since been replicated: "Babies
whose cries got a response more frequently cried less in the last quarter of the
first year of life than those who did not. . . . [This] suggests that trying to interpret
babies' signals, even before they are using them intentionally to communicate, has a
good effect" (p. 80).

In one follow-up study, not just crying, but a number of other infant behaviors,
such as eye contact, gestures such as pointing, and babbles were interpreted in terms
of whether or not they were attempts to communicate. The results?

Mothers who imputed intention to their babies' behaviors reported that their
babies engaged in intentional behavior sooner than reports of babies whose
mothers did not think their baby was using intentional communication.
Why? Because if we interpret a behavior as communicative, we will probably respond to it differently. In other words, the attributions that mothers
make about their babies' behaviors influence how they respond to those
behaviors. Thus, mothers are reinforcing their babies' attempts to communicate with them. (Golinkoff & Hirsh-Pasek, 2000, p. 82)

The implications for early written language communication attempts are clear: attributing meaning to a young child's written language behaviors can have important consequences for a child's written language development. It is vital to assume the children's markings have meaning—and to ask them to tell us those meanings.

As young children progress in their written language, they need what all language learners need: a safe environment in which to take risks, the ability to work through their hypotheses, and the encouragement, appreciation, and respect of the adults who are more experienced written language users.

Finally, young children need the time and space to practice their growing writing prowess. The more practice they have constructing meaning on the written page, the more they will grow in their proficiency.

Drawing and Writing Go Hand in Hand

The study of literacy is all too often a matter of spinning words about words, without looking back to the images that precede words and to the feelings that precede both.

—Leo Lionni

Young children's early drawings are treasured. They are shared with family members to exclaim or chuckle over, they fill scrapbooks, and they hold places of honor on refrigerator doors. Who wouldn't delight in four-year-old Ramon's drawing of his special day at the park with his Mom and his step-Dad Chris? (See Figure 3.1.) Ramon relives his adventures splashing in a puddle, playing on the swings, in the sandbox, and on the monkey bars. But there is so much more going on here than simply a cute example of children's artwork.

Ramon is proud of his carefully gelled spiked haircut. In all the renderings of himself, he makes sure to capture that detail, as well as his new sunglasses. He uses a variety of colors to represent the differences between the mud and the water in the puddle and shows the placement of the different play structures in a kind of intricate map. Though Ramon does not yet use words on his paper, he is making meaning—and communicating—through the symbols he creates.

In order to understand what they see and hear, young children have to attach meaning to the different patterns of light, shape, and color that they see, just as they organize sounds into a linguistic system. The symbols they are creating are intimately tied to children's emerging competence as writers.

FIGURE 3.1

Ramon's drawing:
Family day at the park

Drawing as a Composing Process

Some children's earliest writing appears in the form of letters or created letter shapes, like Carrie sending the note down the stairs to her mom and me (see Chapter 1). But for many children, their drawing *is* their earliest writing. It's important for caregivers and early childhood educators to recognize and honor these drawings for what they are: an important aspect of literacy.

Teacher-researcher Susan Bridge worries that too often drawing is simply portrayed as a kind of "crutch" to be outgrown once the writing process takes hold. "Such a view not only ignores the many ways drawing can aid writing," she points out, "it also ignores the thinking and problem solving that occur when a child draws.

FIGURE 3.2
Eva's writing

Drawing is thinking and deserves more than the frill status that is often given to it" (Bridge, 1988, p. 80).

In her Head Start class, four-year-old Eva is invited to write her stories and she eagerly complies. After completing her paper, she tells her teacher about her piece, a page filled with drawings: "I write rocks. I write me. I'm in the house. This is part of the rainbow. I write a bridge, and I write a big rock. I writed a sun." (See Figure 3.2.)

Another morning, animals are on her mind and her paper. This time, she explains, "I draw a lion. I draw a turtle. I make a penguin. I drawed a giraffe. I had a ticket. I drawed my name." (See Figure 3.3.)

For Eva, drawing and writing are synonymous: they are ways to make her mark and her meaning on the page and communicate her thoughts to her teacher. Her teacher Kelly Petrin knows that writers use detail, so she recognizes the detail in Eva's writing, noting the lines for the lion's mane, the careful color choice for each animal, and the letters that represent the name "Eva" carefully "drawn" on the page.

In Jerome Harste's study of young children's "language stories and literacy lessons" (1984), he noted that he and his research team received a range of responses to the invitation to preschool children to "write a story":

In response to our request, we received a variety of products. Jason drew a picture. Natasha also drew a picture, but not before she had written, "This

FIGURE 3.3
Eva's drawing

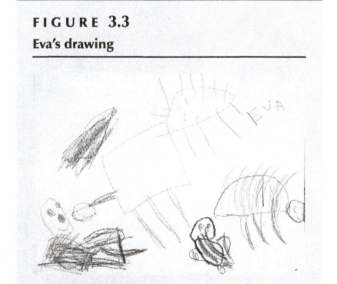

is a puppy." Vincent wrote, "I like candy" using a robust combination of writing and art. . . . *It is important to understand that each child has communicated ideas using graphics as symbols to placehold meaning.* (emphasis added, p. 19)

Paying attention to young children's first writing attempts means honoring the ways they are using the symbols they create to make meaning. And it means paying attention to the content, too; we get a window into their minds, discovering what is happening in their worlds and what is significant to them.

Joseph's drawing is in many ways a typical drawing: a big circle for the head (with eyes and a mouth), and another circle for the body, lines attached to represent limbs. Next to it stands some other creature with what looks like a whole lot of legs (see Figure 3.4). But if we ask Joseph to tell us about his writing, we learn this drawing represents himself with a jellyfish at the beach, a crab in his hand under a bright sun in the sky. He also tells us he has written "part of my name"—and sure enough, you can make out the "J" on the front on his body. That day at the beach is recorded in his memory, and now set on the page to share with others.

FIGURE 3.4

Joseph's day at the beach

Repetition Leads to Understanding

Often, the themes young children write about are repeated, as they depict a favorite subject over and over. In a study of the young writers in her kindergarten classroom, Judy Hilliker discovered a surprising amount of repetition in their pictures (1988)—for example, "Claire drew thirty-seven pictures of the sun and twelve pictures of the sun plus other elements. The sun was the theme of 43 percent of her total drawings from November to March" (p. 15).

More important than simply the notion that children tend to have favorite themes they repeat was Hilliker's discovery of the value of this repetition. She noted that the first written words that accompanied the children's drawings were on the pages that held their significant and repeated themes.

As a result of her study, Hilliker encourages teachers who work with young writers to allow them to explore favorite themes in depth rather than trying something new every day. "Next year, I won't be discouraged by the repetition I find in the children's writing books. Instead of asking them to draw something different, I'll ask them to tell me more about their pictures" (p. 21).

Drawings as Complex Stories

When children create their drawings to communicate their meaning, those pieces they create are not "preliterate"; they are true literacy events. Sometimes an entire story is recorded pictorially. This was the case for Raymond, who had a passionate interest in dinosaurs. The one word on his page is simply a label, each letter copied as a kind of title to the rich narrative he recounts when he "reads" it (see Figure 3.5):

"This is Stegosaurus," he points to the spiky creature in the middle of the paper. "And this is Tyrannosaurus Rex." His finger slides to the left. "And they're fighting, see? Stegosaurus is moving his tail hard." Indeed, I can see the "action lines" that represent the tail moving back and forth.

"And he hits Tyrannosaurus hard and blows his brains out! And

FIGURE 3.5

Raymond's dinosaur story

he knocks his heart right out, too." Raymond traces the lines from the top of the dinosaur's head that show the top being lifted skyward (brains and all!), then moves his finger along the line that follows the trajectory of the heart as it "flies around and goes splat right in Stegosaurus's face!" Raymond's commentary of the story is tied to the marks on the page, which he reads and rereads to his interested audience in the kindergarten classroom.

In her Head Start classroom, Eva also recounts a story using a drawing. Rather than a fictional piece, like Raymond's, Eva crafts a personal narrative about her experience during physical education (see Figure 3.6):

"I am jumping over the stick and hitting the drum," she explains, pointing to the pictures on her page. "I am in the motor room with teacher Joan."

FIGURE 3.6

Eva's narrative

Words and Pictures Working Together

Yet on another day, Eva uses letters as well as her detailed drawing to express her meaning. The class has heard several stories about chameleons, so it isn't surprising that Eva would want to write about them during writing workshop. Her words and pictures together succeed in sharing the information that "chameleon eats a fly" (*KMLEN Fi*) (see Figure 3.7).

Rather than seeing words and images as two very separate systems, early childhood educators are recognizing the importance of how the use of these systems changes depending on the task at hand—and how children use these systems together to complement each other (Harste, Woodward, & Burke, 1984; Hubbard, 1989; Ernst, 1992).

Juan looks up from his writing journal to tell me, *"Hoy, yo voy ir a McDonald's, con mi papa y mi hermano."* (Today I am going to McDonald's with my daddy and brother.)

His drawing is a brilliant rendition of the blocks they will walk together, showing the sidewalk, the fences on either side, and even the steps they will take to reach their

FIGURE 3.7

Eva's story: *Chameleon eats a fly*

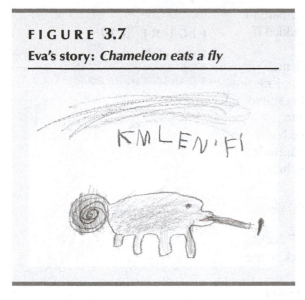

destination. He also uses the well-known golden arch in the shape of an *M*—and carefully depicts even the *M*'s placement on the roof (see Figure 3.8).

Stella is remembering her Halloween experience. I watch her draw in silence; then she begins to explain to me what she's writing about today (see Figure 3.9). "I'm drawin' houses 'cause I'm goin' trick or treating. We're walkin' this way to the house 'cause this light's not on, so we skip this house. On this next house, it's black 'cause the light's on."

Sure enough, on the little square on the door of the first house, Stella has purposely not colored it in. It's "off." On the next house, and all the ones that follow, the little black squares are all shaded in; they're "on"—an important detail that Stella has recorded using symbols.

FIGURE 3.8

Juan's trip to McDonald's

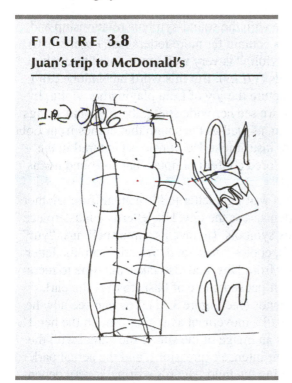

FIGURE 3.9

Stella's Halloween story

Looking at Stella's figures, you wouldn't know the many rich details she has added if you didn't take the time to ask her.

"That girl's hair is way long. It's me!" she tells me. "I have a little half-hood. I'm dressed like a dog. And Ellen had this stupid thing. She's dressed like a football fan. She put makeup on her face. And she had a hat—I'm makin' it. Now I'll make Caitlin's mom. She wasn't dressed up . . . and here's more houses . . ."

"So, it's Halloween. Any words you want to write?" I ask.

"Hallloooooweeeeeennnnn . . . L!" Stella labels her drawing and then turns back to the row of houses to add more details.

Stella and Juan are beginning to label their drawings with letter sounds. As they progress, they will add more and more sounds, while continuing to use their drawings to capture significant details.

FIGURE 3.10

Lola's violin story

Lola is more comfortable with the sound-symbols relationship and her writings contain far more letters (see Figure 3.10). The word "violin" is very well represented through letter sounds (*VILIN*). But this word label alone can't begin to capture the joy of Lola playing her violin. In her picture we see her wide smile, the frets and strings of her violin, as well as the sound that comes from Lola playing her instrument. Her music is captured in the rainbow-colored confetti of notes that surround her as she plays.

Jacob is writing a letter to his penpal from another kindergarten across the city. His letter is a masterpiece of complex symbols. He invents some spellings ("yur" for "your"), copies "dear" and "friend" from the letter he received from Duy, and also takes the time to recreate an action-packed game of basketball at the park with his friends (see Figure 3.11). You can see how he traces the ball's movement as it goes though the net. He also creates an image of the site of the game, with the players, their intense expressions, and the actual park benches lining the field. Jacob's writing is very depen-

FIGURE 3.11

Jacob's basketball game

dent on the picture images; in a sense, the pictures are the verbs of his piece rather than the more static word labels. His spoken explanations to me and his classmates give him a chance to use his oral language to communicate using rich descriptive language.

As five-year-old Jacob becomes comfortable using more letters to show the action, he will likely add these words to his pieces. But that doesn't mean that the drawings are no longer an important element.

Chris, at age six, is also a basketball enthusiast. His written words help him explain a basketball game with far more precision. But in our conference below, note as well his continued reliance on the picture to capture the movement of the game (see Figure 3.12): Chris explains to me that he is writing about a pretend UNH (University of New Hampshire) game. First comes the image in his mind.

"I think in my head what moves would be good on paper. If it doesn't seem like it would look right, I do another one. The pictures can show you what it's all like."

"Well, how do the words help?" I ask.

"If you don't know what's going on, the words can tell you."

I ask him to explain what he means, looking at one page of his ten-page story.

"See, the line shows this player throws the ball up, then there's a rebound. I do the picture first, then I know the words to put down. If I put the words first, it gets confusing."

Chris sees the plot unfolding in his mind. He invents solutions within the medium of drawing to depict the scene—even to show the movement and sequence of events. Then, what can't come across in the picture, he augments with words.

"The second time UNH shot from the foul line, UNH missed and the Huskies caught it."

In Chris' process, it's as if he's not sure how much the drawing can tell until he tries it out; then he fills in the gaps with the written text.

Children like Chris, Juan, Stella, and Lola are writers engrossed in making sense of their worlds, sharing their visions. They are not making random marks on

FIGURE 3.12

Chris' basketball game

their papers, nor are their drawings simply rehearsal for the written text they are composing. Instead, these children are using drawing and writing as tools to create a product to share their images. They are planning and directing no less than I do as an adult writer, deliberately attempting certain effects and posing and solving problems.

Dimension in Literacy: Movement, Space, and Time

Just as infants learning language understand more than they can express orally, young writers have far more advanced concepts than they can communicate with words on the page. Children show ingenuity and complex understanding of the concepts of time, movement and space as they grapple with the constraints of the two-dimensional page. They learn the different perceptual markers—semantic and cultural—that surround them. As they try to transfer the three-dimensional images in their minds to the flat page before them, they rely on both verbal and visual symbols (Hubbard, 1989).

FIGURE 3.13

Lisa "wiped out"

The climax of Lisa's story about her skiing trip is the page where she "wiped out" (see Figure 3.13). Lisa wants to show the progression of her accident and does so by drawing herself both before and after she hits the mogul that caused her to fall. Her drawing and writing require intentional planning to capture the movement of her fall—and her body at different points in time.

Roger writes about the excitement of his first sleepover at a friend's house (see Figure 3.14). He wants to set the time (February) and that it is his friend Barry's house. This he accomplishes with his words. But it is his picture that shows him in the midst of walking to his friend Barry's home. We get to see a top view of him walking next door, down the steps of his house and across the sidewalk. Like Lisa, Roger is very intentional in what he plans and communicates on the page.

I was fortunate to confer with six-year-old Kim in the process of her composing, giving me insights into how she plans and executes her narrative, using both words and picture to capture the dimensions of time and space on her paper.

"You know what happened?" she asks me as she reaches for her writing folder. "My gerbil died. Marshmallow died this weekend."

I'm not quite sure how to react to this update on Marshmallow. Kim's been writing about her gerbils often, chronicling their lives almost daily.

"I'm sorry to hear that, Kim." She nods and smiles in response, grabbing a pencil.

"I can't wait to write about it," she responds (showing the darker side of a writer on a hot topic).

"Mi Jrbldidy on Saturday MsShmlodidy aKoS bKee fegdidy," she writes.

"I'll read it to you. 'My gerbil died on Saturday. Marshmallow died a course, because Fudge died.'" She pauses only a second, then explains matter-of-factly,

FIGURE 3.14

Roger goes to Barry's house

"Must have been old age—they were both twins. Fudge died before Marshmallow, though." She turns back to her composing and adds, "befor Mrshmolo."

"My gerbil died . . ." she rereads, pleased with her work, then reaches for her pencil and circles the word *fegdidy*.

"Know why I circled this? It was my greatest word. I made it with good writing, and fast, too. Now I'll make my greatest pictures." And she sets to work.

When I glance in her direction ten minutes later, I see she is again proudly surveying her work, so I return for an explanation of her drawings.

"I think this *IS* my greatest picture," Kim begins modestly. Above her writing, in the middle of the page is a large square cage, the unfortunate gerbil lying with appropriately stiff legs sticking straight out. Next to his cage is the label "nersited." To the right is a miniature version under the caption, "ordnersen frsited."

"See, this is how it looked: a near-sighted, close-up look . . ." Kim points to the middle of the page, then she runs her finger to the right, "Another scene, far-sighted. That's how it looked when I first came in the room. You know, I thought he might die. I was sleeping over." For the first time, she looks a little sad, but concludes philosophically, "You never know what's going to happen when you go away."

She picks up the pencil again to complete the scene. "Now this will be what's going on outside," she explains, as she draws a long rectangle. "I really don't know because I wasn't there, but I'll draw the window . . . now I'll draw a table with a duck lamp . . . hmmm, there was stuff near it," she muses. She sketches quickly; then, in an aside to me, "It blows air out so you won't have to dust around the house."

She returns again to her rendering of the dead Marshmallow, adding lines to represent the wood chips in his cage, and the water bottle hanging from the top (see Figure 3.15).

"He was going like this at the time," she demonstrates, turning on her side and sticking her arms out straight before her.

She might have added more to her piece, but it's 9:00, and Kim has signed up to share her writing in the author's chair. When she has read her entire piece to the class, hands fly up.

"Why did you write about it?" Jill wants to know.

"I just wanted to write about it because I like to write about my gerbils."

After several more questions, Bobby shyly raises his hand. "It's sad," he says quietly.

Kim looks at him, pauses. "I know."

It would be difficult to list the many skills that Kim's work exemplified that morning. Besides her sophisticated use of language and manipulation of symbols, two crucial elements of her writing process are evident: intentionality and the ability to be self-reflective. These two skills are often excluded as necessary for writing development in young children, yet they are at the heart of writing and drawing as thinking processes.

FIGURE 3.15
Kim's gerbil died

Working with Young Children as They Draw and Write

The logic by which we teach is not always the logic by which children learn.

—Glenda Bissex

Educators of young children can learn much from Glenda Bissex's advice to look to the logic that children are employing as they write. The best way to gain insight into these processes is to pull up a chair alongside children, watch them as they work, and ask them genuine questions based on their drawing and writing. Not only does this give us as educators assessment information so we can plan how to best support our students and nudge them forward, it is also a wonderful way to help students use metacognitive processes, honing their abilities to be reflective and to explain their thinking.

The process of having conferences with young writers is very much like conferring with writers of any age: we listen, and have a genuine conversation with the author, asking questions about both content and process. My conferences with Kim and Chris as they drew and wrote are examples of the kind of conferences that give children a chance to show their intentions, discover their process, and communicate their messages.

In these classroom situations, the children are also writing for genuine audiences: their classmates, their teacher, and other members of their classroom community. The wider audience helps nudge children's thinking forward, as they have chances to explain their work to interested peers. Bobby can express his empathy for the death of Kim's pet gerbil because he has heard her stories about her pets over time and knows this is an important part of her life. Kim has the chance to work out the meaning of this event in her conversations as well as in her writing and drawing.

As we shift our lens for viewing children's early literacy, we can begin to see the ingenuity and playfulness of their work—of their pictures as well as their words. Drawing is not just for children who cannot yet write fluently, and creating pictures is not just part of rehearsal for real writing. Images at any age are part of the serious business of making meaning—partners with words for communicating what is in our minds.

Writing Conference Principles

41

Working
with Young
Children as
They Draw
and Write

- *Let the child lead.* We lean in and listen to any child as we confer, trusting that they can begin by helping us understand where they are in their writing, and possibilities for what they might learn next.

- *Know the history of the child, and the history of the piece of writing.* We know the passions of each child in the classroom, with many children repeating a few crucial themes in their writing—family, favorite hobbies, friends, animals, toys. When we are stuck in a conference, we can often find a way into the writing through these passions and our shared history as writers.

- *Assume the child has something to communicate.* There is always logic behind a child's writing, words and ideas, no matter how confused we might feel when we read a particular draft—it's just a matter of finding out what in the child's experience has led them to their current thinking, talking and symbol-making on the page.

- *Be patient, and respect silence.* It is hard for us at times to slow down and be "in the moment" with an individual child—there are often other children tugging at our sleeves, no matter how often we admonish everyone to respect the space and time of their classmates in conferences. But we need to slow down, listen, and most important, give the children all the time they need to formulate thoughts, or think through just the right word, picture or phrase to capture their new ideas.

- *Write down the child's ideas in a notebook or at the bottom of the page.* This isn't dictation, as much as our attempt to ensure we can remember the child's narrative in their own words.

- *Look for the teaching moment.* It might be as subtle as nudging a child toward including more details in their drawing, or as explicit as guiding a child to write a new letter. Some of the most important teaching moments for us celebrate what the child has done well. Success breeds success, and children aren't always aware of the new skills and strategies they are mastering and might use in other contexts.

- *Keep it short.* We try to meet with as many children as possible each day in the classroom, circulating through the room and checking in as children write. Some conferences are just a quick sentence or two of support. Others include a few minutes of pulling up a chair and watching as a child writes, asking questions about their drawings or words. It is a rare thirty-minute conferring session where we don't manage to check in with all twenty children in the class.

- *Include follow-up.* When we leave a conference, the child and teacher both know what is coming next—continuing in a draft, starting a new piece, fleshing out a drawing, or publishing the writing in some form.

Source: Brenda Power and Ruth Shagoury (Choice Literacy, 2006, www.choiceliteracy.com)

Understanding Young Spellers

F ive-year-old Carmen looks down at the paper in front of her then rolls her
eyes up to the ceiling, tapping her pencil. "Double-u," she says under her
breath. "Double-u. How do you make a double-u . . ."

Julie lifts her own crayon from the page and turns to her friend, "I don't know
how to make a double-u, but I can spell it! It begins with a D."

John tugs on his Head Start teacher Kelly Petrin's sleeve.

"Teacher Kelly, did you know I know how to spell circle?"

"No!"

"Yes, come and watch me." Kelly watches as John uses his crayon to draw a
large purple circle.

Carmen, Julie, and John are very young writers, beginning to construct meaning
on the page through the marks they make. Already, they know something of the
concept of spelling and are grappling with its relationship to writing. They are actively
involved in their own recreation of written language; they are inventing spelling.

Writing and Spelling

Invented spelling is a term that seeks to capture the underlying language knowledge that young children are relying on when they use their own spellings to construct knowledge through print. This term was first used in 1971 by two researchers who investigated young spellers' developmental patterns (Chomsky, 1971; Read, 1971).

Since then, it has come into mainstream educational usage, but is still often used incorrectly. Sandra Wilde (1992) addresses a common misconception about invented spelling in her landmark research study. When asked by teachers and parents, "Is invented spelling merely a euphemism for *misspelling*?" her answer is a resounding "No.":

> "[E]uphemism" means that an unpleasant truth is being glossed over, imply-
> ing that the term "invented spelling" is an attempt to excuse error. But this
> is not the case. Insisting on a term like misspelling or spelling error suggests
> that the writer was aiming for the correct spelling but failed, presumably
> through ignorance or carelessness. This does not accurately describe the
> process . . . Invention is not a failure to achieve convention, but a step on the
> road to achieving it." (Wilde, 1992, p. 3)

Chomsky's, Read's, and Wilde's research all demonstrate that invented spelling represents attempts to use writing as a way to transcribe sounds. As such, it shows an understanding of the principle of spelling. Subsequent research has demonstrated that young children's invented spellings are systematic and evolving, that spellings progress toward more complete representation of sound, and that children have no trouble making the transition to conventional spelling when it is required of them (Gerritz, 1974; Beers & Henderson, 1977; Graves, 2002).

With invented spelling, there is a typical developmental progression. One key tenet to keep in mind is that children begin with a larger, more global knowledge about spelling and then move to a more specific understanding of how their own culture's particular system is organized. When children move from the scribble stage to alphabetic writing, although they do tend to do so in fairly predictable stages, it is important not to see these stages as a required route for development. Margaret Hughes and Dennis Searle list three main cautions against seeing stages in spelling as clear-cut and unvarying:

1. What children do in terms of spelling is more complex than applying a particular strategy to every word in every situation.

2. Children often use strategies associated with earlier stages of development when
   grappling with new vocabulary or unfamiliar features in a word.

3. While most observations of children's spelling growth has a clear sound-
   based connection, there are children who use sight more than sound as well as

hearing-impaired children who do not typically use sound as the entry route to understanding spelling. (Hughes & Searle, 1997)

With this important caveat in mind, there are still common patterns, trends and understandings about spelling that are recognizable as part of children's journey as spellers. Table 4.1 shows a typical invented spelling developmental progression, leading to conventional spelling, with samples as illustration. (For larger illustrations of this chart, see Appendix A.)

TABLE 4.1 Developmental Progression in Invented Spelling

1. Random letters to represent meaning:
   ("I just write 'em; I don't read 'em.")

Nicole's random letters

2. Labeling with beginning phonetic spelling: Most often initial consonants, then initial and ending, but sometimes the letters that a child knows from her own name or from letters with clear sound-symbol correspondence (*I S R*).
   Growing sound-symbol correspondence.
   A combination of how words sound and how words look. More use of vowels.

Bianca's "sun"   **Brooke's "ladybug"**

3. Moving toward convention: Use of multistrategies for spelling. Further refinement where letters represent more sounds in words. Some words are invented, and others are remembered.

Amelia's "butterfly"   **Lacey's "me and my dog walking in the park"**

4. Further refinement where letters represent more sounds in words. Some words are invented and others are remembered.

Chris' "Chicks like to stay warm. They grow new feathers."

Conventional Spelling

1. Random Letters to Represent Meaning

The first stage in invented spelling is when children put down strings of letters that are simply combinations of letters they know how to make, as Nicole did in the sample shown in the chart. Literacy researcher Anne Haas Dyson tells the story of a young boy who was writing independently line after line of letters. When Anne asked him to read his writing to her, he looked up and said, "Hey, I just write 'em. I don't read 'em!" (2004). At this stage, children know that the letters represent meaning to others, even if they don't yet know what that meaning is.

Working with children in this phase of development: Children need to know that you are interested in the writing and drawing they are doing. As in any discussion with a child about his or her writing, it helps to begin by asking what they are writing about. Often, children will describe the picture, or "read" back their writing, using the paper as a kind of prop for the story they are telling. On the other hand, children will sometimes simply tell you that they can't read yet. In this case, I urge children to tell me what they were thinking about as they wrote, describe their drawing, or tell me who they would like to show this piece of writing to. Another strategy is to show interest in their process, talking about the letters themselves: "How do you decide which letters you're going to write?" "You know a lot of letters. How did you learn them?" or, "What letters will you write next?"

2. Labeling with Beginning Phonetic Spelling

Even without instruction in letters, children typically begin by labeling their drawings with consonant sounds, usually using beginning or ending letters. They most often use letters from their names, or letters with clear sound-symbol correspondence.

Bianca's and Brooke's examples shown in Table 4.1 demonstrate that it is easy to read back these spellings (Bianca's *SN* for sun and Brooke's *LDB* for ladybug), especially with the drawings that are part of the writing that is represented on the page.

Working with children in this phase of development: With young children like Bianca and Brooke, it is easy to see that they understand the sound-symbol relationship and can use letters to represent the sounds in the words they hear. Araceli was another child whom I had observed writing letters to label her drawings. In the transcript below, you'll notice that as I talk with her about her story, I encourage her to add more letter sounds that she knows:

Ruth: So, Araceli, tell me what you're writing today.

Araceli: Me and my sister.

Ruth: What's your sister's name?

Araceli: Carolyn.

Ruth: Oh, so this is an apple tree? What's gonna happen next?

Araceli: I'm gonna write names. (She writes *Araceli.*)

Ruth: I know you know how to write Araceli. Do you know how to write Carolyn? Or what sounds Carolyn might start with?

Araceli: K.

Ruth: Great! You can write that right next to it in case somebody was looking at this, then they would know who that is. Looks like you both have necklaces on. You have matching necklaces?

Araceli: (nods)

Ruth: How about the tree? Do you want to write anything for tree?

Araceli: Tree . . . *T*! (She writes *T*)

Ruth: Uh huh . . . Any other sounds you hear in tree?

Araceli: Trrr . . . *r R*??

Ruth: Sure, go ahead.

In this case, Araceli just needs the encouragement of someone sitting next to her, and talking with her to experiment with more letter sounds (see Figure 4.1).

José is a slightly different story. I haven't yet seen him write letters with his drawings, but I've seen him listening in on other children's conferences, and sense his eagerness to take a risk. I've watched him write his name with confidence, and

FIGURE 4.1
Araceli's writing

play with the letter puzzles in the room. In the following conference, I do a little direct instruction to nudge him toward what he seems ready for.

José has drawn a field of flowers and shows them to me. I slowly say the word, "flowers," and ask José what he hears. "*f*?" he queries.

"Yes, that's what I hear, too. Do you know what letter makes the sound?"

José shakes his head no.

"Do you want to learn?"

Silence again, but with a big nod and smile.

I show him how to make an *f.* We practice together several *f*'s and his smile gets wider (see Figure 4.2). Because this letter sound grew from his own writing—a drawing of flowers—he is more likely to remember what he has learned. As a teacher,

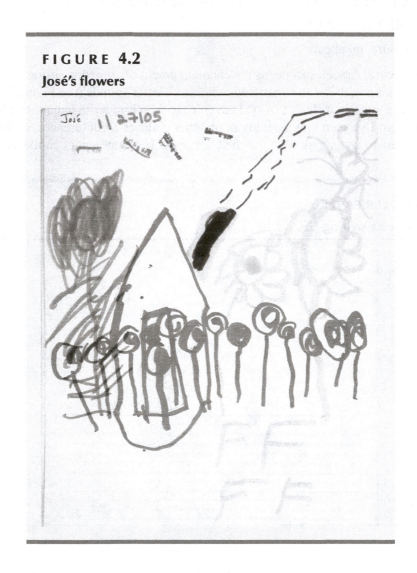

FIGURE 4.2

José's flowers

my next step is to check in with him and see if he can read back his writing, and if he uses the *f* correctly in future writing.

Once children have made that leap to understanding that they can use a range of symbols—letters and drawings—to make meaning on the page, they often make great leaps, adding more and more sounds, like Griffith's story about his cat: MCLN ("my cat likes night"), Kim's tale of catching butterflies in "summer time" (SRM TIM), or Matt's remembrance of the alligator he saw at the zoo: ALGATr. (See Figures 4.3, 4.4, and 4.5.)

There are other alphabets that use a sound-symbol correspondence, of course. Marina, a young Russian speaker, used Cyrillic as well as English symbols in her invented spelling. As Christmas approached, she drew a picture of the

FIGURE 4.3

Griffith's cat story

FIGURE 4.4

Kim's summertime

FIGURE 4.5

Matt's alligator

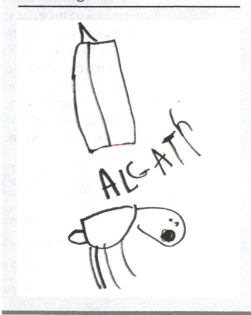

tree they were decorating at home, and used many sounds as a label for her story about Christmas (see Figure 4.6). Marina consistently uses the P symbol to represent the /r/ sound, which is the correct correspondence in Russian (Christmas: KPCMaC).

3. Growing Sound-Symbol Correspondence

When children have more time to practice writing, they use everything at their disposal to add more and more letters to their writing. As their understanding of sound-symbol relationships grows, they use their graphophonemic knowledge to spell in three ways:

FIGURE 4.6
Marina's Christmas story

spelling the way it sounds; spelling the way it looks; and spelling the way it means (Harste, Woodward, & Burke, 1984). They also use combinations of these strategies.

Stella is moving into using more sounds as well as whole sentences of thought. I sit down next to her as she writes one morning, drawing big circles on her paper. I'm not quite sure what the circles represent, but she is always intentional in her work. So, I ask her to tell me about her writing.

"It's jewelry. A kit I got for Christmas."

Sure enough, her words explain her drawing: THEES MY GOY I LYE PK I MAD. This is my jewelry. I like it because I made it (see Figure 4.7).

Working with children in this phase of development: Children like Stella are in a written vocabulary spurt, very similar to the fast-mapping stage of oral language

Early Spelling Strategies

The way it sounds: JRF (giraffe)

The way it looks: FRO (for)

The way it means: WASAPANATAEM (once upon a time)

Combination: ACWQEUM MIY (my aquarium)

learning (see Chapter 1). Just as in oral language, children at this stage of writing development are ripe for more learning, soaking up the words and sounds they see and hear around them. The more opportunities they have to experiment with making these sounds and committing them to paper the more efficiently they will continue to learn.

For many adults and caregivers, the temptation at this stage is to spell the words for the children. This "help" from adults can actually slow the child's growth. By depending on someone else to tell them what letters to put down next, the child does not have the chance to truly work on phonic connections to the letters. It is vital for the children to hear and make those connections themselves. They will be much better able to read back their own inventions, moving them from *encoding* their words to actually *decoding* them as well. Instead of spelling for the children, the adult role is to be supportive in encouraging them to say words slowly, and take risks in putting down the sounds they hear, even if they are not all correct.

Children in this period also benefit from working independently and with other children, rather than relying on adults to take dictations of the child's words. The problem with dictations at this point is that children will soon learn it is much quicker to just tell their words to someone who writes everything down than to work—and sometimes struggle—to compose the words themselves. Besides the lack of practice with individual sounds, the practice of dictation at this stage will get in the way of a child's independence as a writer.

4. Moving toward Convention: Further Refinement

As Chris observes the chicks hatching and growing in his first-grade classroom, he keeps track of their development in his writing journal (See sample in Table 4.1: *Chicks like to sta worm they gro noo fathers.*) His writing shows that he is clearly moving toward convention in his spelling:

- He uses digraphs such as "ch" and "th" correctly.

- He knows some common sight words: they; to; like.

- He shows an understanding of phonic principles in his invented spellings: "oo" and the long vowels *A* and *O*.

Besides adding digraphs and more vowels, children in this stage start to show they

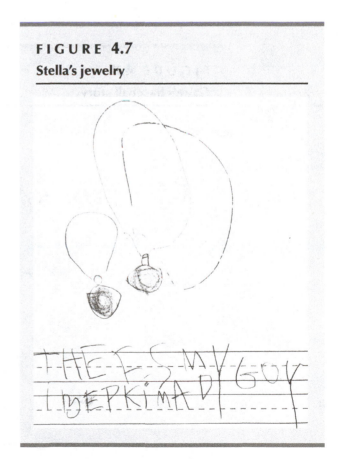

FIGURE 4.7
Stella's jewelry

have a knowledge of morphemes such as "ing," "er," and "ed." They are also adding more visual recall to their spelling strategies.

This added knowledge and willingness to use both recall and invention in writing words allows children to write longer and more complex stories. Gabe's story of a Red Sox versus Cleveland Indians game shows his many strengths in writing words, sounds, and using his pictures to make meaning:

1. the Boston red sox and the clevlend indins are playing baseball aganst each other

2. the red sox hit the ball

3. the outfelder cot the Ball

4. the red sox misst the ball

5. but the nekst time the red sox hit a home run

And this is only the beginning of Gabe's 27-page magnum opus! Even in these five pages, the list of what he knows about written language is stunning. (See Figure 4.8.)

FIGURE 4.8

Gabe's baseball story

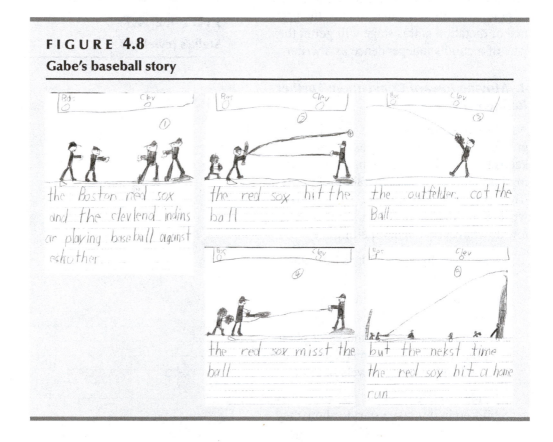

Working with children in this phase of development: Too often, rather than focusing on this amazing bank of knowledge, adults look first at what the child *doesn't* know instead of what she *does*. The best help we can give children at this stage—and at all stages of their language development—is to look at their strengths, point out their knowledge and understandings, and build from there.

Children who show they are adding more spelling skills to their repertoire and moving toward convention benefit from chances to talk with adults about both the content of their writing, and the craft of writing itself. It can be helpful to share the way published authors of picture books write words and use drawings and illustrations. Young spellers can also talk about how they make choices and decisions in their written work—why they chose to spell a word a certain way, or how they learned it. As at all stages, continued practice based on ideas and stories they want to write about is crucial.

What Does This Mean for Classroom Instruction?

Many teachers and parents think of spelling as a rote skill and assume growth in spelling depends on memorization and an emphasis on correctness. But current research has shown that, like learning to talk, learning to spell is a language function. Both depend on invention, imitation, interaction, and risk-taking (Bissex, 1980; Hughes & Searle, 1997; Wilde, 1992).

From the samples in this chapter, you can see that working with spelling through context can provide growth toward convention as children write. Their "errors" are not accidental, but reflect their systems of knowledge. As Bissex stresses, "Spelling ability grows from understanding a system and cannot be accounted for as the product of memorized lists of unpredictably spelled words" (Bissex, 1980, p. 111).

How can educators help create meaningful spelling instruction based on what we know about children's developmental growth? The key is in turning to the children themselves as our informants, learning about their own processes and understandings. One major change in instruction with school-aged children, for example, has been to draw the words to be learned from children's own writing instead of from lists supplied by spelling texts (Graves, 2002).

First-grade teacher Patricia McLure built from her students' knowledge by crafting a program based on words they knew how to spell and creating minilessons from the children's chosen words. (See page 55.)

Even with younger children, it is important to build from their knowledge and understanding. Kindergarten teacher Andie Cunningham invites her students to create the alphabet charts that grace the walls (see poster samples, Figures 4.9, 4.10, 4.11). Each child creates at least one letter and illustrates it with drawings and magazine cutouts of words that represent that sound. Because the children

FIGURE 4.9
Jacob's letter poster

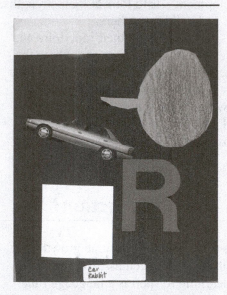

FIGURE 4.10
Alma's letter poster

FIGURE 4.11
Lola's letter poster

themselves create the poster symbols, they are genuine tools for the community. Jacob's poster for the letter *R* is illustrated by a rabbit and a ca(R); these are sounds he knows and can tell other children in the class if they look to his letter page. With commercially published posters and pages, the images children "read" may not match the sounds for the words they are seeking. For example, five-year-old Louisa was frustrated as she looked at a commercial letter sheet, seeking the sound /B/ to label her drawing of a bunny. She found the picture of a bunny, but it illustrated the letter *R*.

It also helps to invite children into our spelling assessment process. Kindergarten teacher Andie Cunningham keeps a sheet in each child's writing folder with the letters of the alphabet without illustrations. When she sees a child using a letter in context, she highlights that letter with a marker, sharing what she is doing with the child. If she teaches a child a letter, she places a check mark on the letter page—a reminder to follow up to see if the child is able to use it after being taught.

If you ask a class of first-graders what they know how to spell, be prepared, because they know a lot. The variety of words in their spelling vocabulary far exceeds any spelling list we might assign to them.

In January, I started by asking the children in my class to spell a word each day. It could be any word of their choice. We have this spelling lesson each morning sitting in a circle in the classroom meeting area. When I started, I thought of it as a positive way to reinforce the idea that there are conventional spellings for words. Well, it accomplishes that, but a lot more happens as well. Our spelling time has become a time to share experiences, affirm friendships, learn about geography, phonetic patterns, and hear about family members.

In looking back through our master list where I record everyone's words, I see lots of names. Children have spelled names of people, cities, and countries, book titles, soccer teams, brands of sneakers, and names of pets. It becomes a public announcement of friendship when one child spells the name of a friend and the friend spells his name in return. The children share some news or an experience by spelling a name. Tara had a new cousin born recently and it took her three days to learn to spell Jacqueline. Katherine spelled Epcot Center after her trip to Florida and Barry spelled Ireland and Bunratty Castle after his trip.

Some children followed word categories. Chris spelled a color word each day and Noa spelled a number word. Jill got interested in birds and practiced their names at home and at school. She spelled robin, cardinal, goldfinch, and bluebird. Then Chris became interested, so Jill helped him learn some birds' names.

Many times the children's words lead us into a short phonics lesson. It's easy to look through the list and pick out some words with the short *a* sound or ones with a long vowel and the silent *e*. One day, Nathan spelled "moving," Bobby spelled "missing," and Barry spelled "jumping." That was the day we talked about adding *-ing* to a word.

Long words were popular for a while. *Mississippi* was spelled by several children. Then Adrienne added *xylophone* to her list, Dwayne spelled *kangaroo,* Barry spelled *battleship,* and Kimberly learned *television.*

There seems to be no shortage of ideas. The list will continue to grow until the last day of school in June.

Kindergarten teachers at Andie's school also chart their students' growth toward convention by asking them to spell a list of words at different points in the year. The intent is not for children to spell them correctly, but for teachers to chart their growth. (See Figure 4.12.)

FIGURE 4.12

Spelling Growth Samples: Matt, Marina, Lola, and Juan

Kindergarten Writing Assignment / Teacher Recording Form

Name: _____ Matt _____

Directions: Give the child a sheet of paper. Have the child write their name first. Demonstrate how to say a word slowly by using a common word such as "mom". Then say each word and <u>ask the child to say the word slowly</u> and write the sounds he/she hears. Record the child's exact response on this recording form. Attach the child's paper to this recording form.

Date: 1/20   Date: 4/2   Date: 5/8

rat		rΛ	rA
buzz	S(?)	BS	BAZ
I	I	I	I
kiss		S	KTS
game	M	MΛ	gAM
a	A	A	A
sleep	∽	2L	SLEP
yellow	O	LO	ELO
	5/22	12/22	18/22

Kindergarten Writing Assignment / Teacher Recording Form

Name: _____ Marina _____

Directions: Give the child a sheet of paper. Have the child write their name first. Demonstrate how to say a word slowly by using a common word such as "mom". Then say each word and <u>ask the child to say the word slowly</u> and write the sounds he/she hears. Record the child's exact response on this recording form. Attach the child's paper to this recording form.

Date: 1/19   Date: 4/5   Date: 5/9

rat		PAT	PAT
buzz	Z	BAZZZ	BZ
I		A:H	i
kiss		KHS	KC
game		EA	AM
a	AM	A	A
sleep		SLHP	CIEN
yellow	YO	HAO	EiO
	4/22	12/22	16/22

Kindergarten Writing Assignment / Teacher Recording Form

Name: _____ Lola _____

Directions: Give the child a sheet of paper. Have the child write their name first. Demonstrate how to say a word slowly by using a common word such as "mom". Then say each word and <u>ask the child to say the word slowly</u> and write the sounds he/she hears. Record the child's exact response on this recording form. Attach the child's paper to this recording form.

Date: 1/20   Date: 3/21   Date: 5/1

rat	RT	RT	rAT
buzz	B	BZ	BZ
I	i	I	i
kiss	S	TS	KSS
game	A	AB	AM
a	—	Λ	A
sleep	S	SLEP	SLEP
yellow		LO	LO
	7/22	14/22	17/22

Kindergarten Writing Assignment / Teacher Recording Form

Name: _____ Juan _____

Directions: Give the child a sheet of paper. Have the child write their name first. Demonstrate how to say a word slowly by using a common word such as "mom". Then say each word and <u>ask the child to say the word slowly</u> and write the sounds he/she hears. Record the child's exact response on this recording form. Attach the child's paper to this recording form.

Date: 1/23   Date: 3/21   Date: 5/9

rat	△	I	R
buzz	.	•T	B
I		L	L
kiss		I	S
game		IS	M
a		A	A
sleep		SOSO	S
yellow	OZ	tO	O
	1/22	5/22	7/22

The following are wonderful, practical references for spelling instruction based on language acquisition and development principles:

You Kan Red This!: Spelling and punctuation for whole language classrooms K–6. Sandra Wilde. 1991. Portsmouth, NH: Heinemann. This comprehensive handbook for teachers documents spelling and punctuation development in kindergarten through sixth-grade classrooms. Throughout the book, there are many examples and demonstrations of ways to integrate spelling into writing instruction. I appreciate the thoughtful marriage of theory and practice in this accessible text for teachers.

The violent E and other tricky sounds: Learning to spell from kindergarten through grade six. Margaret Hughes and Dennis Searle. 1997. Portland, ME: Stenhouse. Teachers and childcare workers will appreciate the detailed theoretical study of how children grow toward conventional spelling. This text is particularly useful for teachers who wish to monitor their students' strategies and progress as spellers and plan lessons that meet the needs of the individual readers and writers in their classroom.

Spelling inquiry: How one school caught the mnemonic plague. Kelly Chandler and the Mapleton Teacher-Research Group. 1999. Portland, ME: Stenhouse. This is an exciting text on two levels. It tells the story of a school that decided to have a school-wide focus on spelling. As readers, we see the ways they worked with their students across grade levels, as well as the discussions that propelled their teaching and inquiry. The other fascinating narrative tells the story of how a school created a teacher-research inquiry group that sustained their questions and brought together their school community on a deep and professional level. The book is filled with research and practical suggestions for the teaching of spelling as well as tips for creating and sustaining teacher-research inquiry groups.

Spelling instruction that makes sense. Jo Phenix and Doreen Scott-Dunne. 1991. Markham, Ontario: Pembroke Publishers. What a wonderful resource in providing alternatives to weekly spelling lists! The authors stress how spellers learn to construct words, not merely memorize them. Like reading and writing, spelling is about making meaning, and making sense of patterns. I especially appreciate the useful advice for helping emergent spellers.

Conventions and Beyond

E   rick is hard at work on his epic tale of the family trip to the coast. When I slide into the seat next to him, he offers to read his piece, carefully explaining the pictures as well.

"See? This is a back view of me over the fence." He picks up his pencil and carefully writes, "SO I HAD TO GO THO THE FANS."

After a brief discussion of his piece, I point to the last sentence. "Erick, I notice you leave spaces between the words in your writing."

Erick nods. "Yeah, you need to so you can read the words back."

Roger inches closer, glancing at Erick's paper, then his own story.

"Some kids don't leave spaces," Erick goes on, "so they have trouble when they want to read it."

Now Jenny looks down at her paper where a row of letters marches across the paper. "I can't read this back, 'cause I wrote it Friday," she confesses. "Nobody can read it, I don't think."

Erick has discovered an important tool for his writing—a convention that helps him decipher his own texts more easily. This is a convention that is shared by the adult published authors the children read as well as the writers in his classroom community. Learning the conventions of writing is similar to learning the agreed-upon spellings in a writing system: children experiment, create, and learn from the culture of which they are a part.

What Are Conventions?

Written language systems have evolved to include rules of expression to make communication easier. These rules, such as punctuation and capitalization, are tools to make written thought more understandable. They work for a community of language users because they are socially agreed upon. When Erick and his friends come to understand that leaving spaces between words helps everyone read back writing, they are reaping the "fringe benefits" of conventions.

When convention is the only lens that educators use, however, there is a real danger of elevating these surface structures over meaning in written work. Further, we fail to see linguistic growth as continuous after convention has been reached. Just as with every aspect of writing development, we can learn most when we seek to understand the evolving hypotheses that children are experimenting with in their written language.

One morning in Patricia McLure's first-grade spelling time (see Chapter 4), Matt chose to spell the word "bear."

"Bear. Capital B-e-a-r."

Rather than saying, "No, we don't capitalize bear," Patricia took an extra moment to probe deeper.

"Matt, why did you say capital B?"

"'Cause it's the name of an animal," Matt responded promptly.

Matt has learned that we *do* capitalize names—names of people, places, days of the week and months. He is overgeneralizing this written language convention but showing a true understanding of it.

Because Patricia understands Matt's hypothesis, she can use this as a teaching moment. "That's good thinking, Matt. But it's really a kind of animal, not the name of an animal, so we don't use capitals for kinds of animals, like bears or chickens or dogs. So can you spell it again?"

"Bear. b-e-a-r."

Anne Haas Dyson, in her ethnographic study of first-grade literacy events, examines how as children learn the written word, there is an important intersection between language, literacy, and social context (Dyson, 2004).

She also writes about the "capital *B*" in an important vignette involving six-year-old Ezekial.

Today is my mom's
Brthday

Ezekial begins his journal entry one day with these words. As Dyson notes, at first glance this is a simple telling of a personal event with an "impressive apostrophe and a misplaced capital *B*" (Dyson, 2004, p. 8).

On closer examination, Dyson found that Ezekial was responding to a recent minilesson his teacher, Mrs. K, had conducted. As she wrote about buying her daughter a Halloween costume, Mrs. K. called attention to her spaces between words and the use of a capital *H* on Halloween (because "it is a holiday"). When she had finished, the children in the class shared their stories of Halloween costumes or treat-or-treating plans. Except Ezekial, who told about his mother's birthday and the family plans to celebrate. But Ezekial was not off-topic, as Dyson and Mrs. K. originally thought:

> Back at their seats, many children began to write about Halloween, and Ezekial began to write about his mother's "Birthday." When Mrs. K. inquired about that capital B on birthday, he explained that birthday was "the name of a holiday." "It's a special day at your house, isn't it, when it's someone's birthday?" she replied. "But is it a special day at Tionna's house because it's your mother's birthday?"
>
> Ezekial gave her a wide-eyed, somber look. "Probably not," said Mrs. K. in a sympathetic voice. She explained that a holiday would be a special day, not only at his house, but at other people's houses, too. Ezekial erased the apparently self-involved capital B and substituted the more socially sensitive lower case one. (p. 9)

In Ezekial's case, the story did not end here. As Dyson learned more about Ezekial's standing in the classroom, she learned that he was "writing himself into the classroom conversation about holidays" because his family did not believe in celebrating Halloween. As the rest of the class took part in talking and writing about this holiday event, he found a way to use conventions to allow himself to participate in the classroom "public" conversation.

Dyson argues convincingly that "that capital B on birthday was an indicator of his social desire to be included. In a similar way, other children may appropriate and blend linguistic, textual, and experiential resources from out-of-school social worlds in order to participate in school" (Dyson, 2004, p. 12).

In support of her claim, Dyson shows a variety of examples where children are making hypotheses for their use of convention, not simply misusing convention. For instance, in some texts from the classroom library, book characters shout out their words in capital letters; the children, in turn, borrow this convention in their own writing to make their words "louder."

The important point to keep in mind as we explore young children's evolving understanding and use of written conventions is the children's "alertness to print in and out of school, acknowledging what children themselves notice about the graphic options used by composers of signs, cards, comics, websites, books of all kinds, and on and on" (Dyson, 2004, p. 14). In other words, children are testing their hypotheses about how written language looks; we can learn much from trying to understand these hypotheses rather than simply "correct" them. Simple mastery of rules doesn't serve us as educators because we miss an opportunity to understand how children are growing toward convention. And it doesn't serve the child, who can come to believe that these rules are simply arbitrary and not powerful ways to help make meaning clearer and at times to achieve more nuances through print.

A Kid's-Eye View of Punctuation

Besides use of capitalized and lowercase letters, young children are also developing concepts of the conventions of punctuation. In their research of preschool children, Ferreiro and Teberosky (1982) discovered that the children they studied gradually came to discriminate numbers and letters from the various punctuation marks of their culture. Ferreiro and Teberosky note a clearly developmental process from not distinguishing punctuation marks from letters and numbers to, ultimately, not only understanding the differences but assigning labels and functions to the different marks.

Other researchers, such as Edelsky (1983) and Calkins (1980), found that children moved from idiosyncratic usage to more conventional usage over time. Significantly, Calkins notes that children "developed an intuitive sense for the nuances of punctuation" through practice in their writing, without needing to be dependent on rules.

The earliest marks children use in their writing other than letters tend to be exclamation marks and question marks (Bissex, 1980; Calkins, 1980). Five-year-old Song used both in her story about her sister (see Figure 5.1). When I asked her to tell me about her writing, she told me it said, "My sister is happy! She excited!" Song writes using both Chinese characters and letters from the alphabet. While her letters don't yet correspond to the sounds, she uses them to placehold meaning and even writes the label "no" (*ON*) next to part of her drawing she has crossed

FIGURE 5.1

Song's sister is happy!

FIGURE 5.2

Hakim's ski story

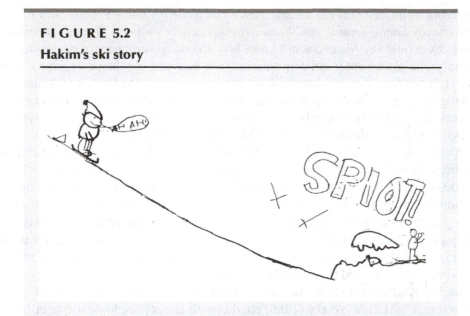

out. And she understands conventions that put emphasis on what is written. Here, she has underlined her letters and surrounded them with "marks" of excitement: an exclamation mark and a question mark. Song, like many other children I have observed, wants her words to "shout" off the page and uses conventions to help get that across.

A page from Hakim's skiing story provides a very graphic example of use of a text convention to emphasize the sound words can make (see Figure 5.2). As one figure in the drawing, Hakim, looks on and laughs, his brother skis through a mound of snow. The "SPLOT!" is not only emphasized with the convention of an exclamation point, but the words themselves are enlarged, outlined, and given dimension to emphasize the sound at the point of impact.

Children also begin to show their understanding of other conventions through experiments with their use, even if they don't yet quite understand placement. Take a look at Alana's story about her ability to write the names of members of her family (see Figure 5.3). (Translation: *I can write my father's*

FIGURE 5.3

Alana's family story

> I can raeiyty MY faeiy's
> Name. and I can raeiyty
> MY old'dly Name.
> and I can raeiyty MY
> ulcsyl's Name. and I can
> raeiyty MY aieye's Name.
> and I can raeiyty MY
> a cnyeiay's Name.

name. And I can write my [?]'s name. And I can write my uncle's name. And I can write my auntie's name. And I can write my cousin's name.) Through a deficit model, we would say Alana doesn't know how to use apostrophes for possession correctly: the placement is not conventional, nor does she use the possessive *s*. But if we shift our lens to note what she *does know,* we can see the ways that Alana is growing in her understanding of the use of apostrophes for possession. For example, she uses the mark only in words that require the possessive, not randomly sprinkled through her story. This shows a wonderful grasp of the use of this convention.

Alana also shows a beginning understanding of the use of periods at the end of sentences. Though she does not end her sentences with periods consistently, when she does use a period, it is correctly placed. Again, she demonstrates that her use is not random, but based on her hypotheses of the uses of this particular convention. Many young children who are "taught" the use of periods before they are ready simply place them randomly or, more often, at the end of every line, even if it is not the end of a sentence. Examples such as Alana's and Song's show the importance of following children's lead to teachable moments.

As Jeff Anderson stresses, the key is "loving students' errors, loving their approximations. Lev Vygotsky (1986) taught us all about pseudo-concepts or budding theories based on initial impressions. Kids have a reason for doing what they do, even if it is flawed" (2005, p. 4).

. . . And Beyond

There are also many marks on the page that help the reader make sense of the communication, which are seldom "taught," yet children are grappling with them at the same time they wrestle with spelling and punctuation. Certain conventions, such as cartoon-type action lines and multiple drawings to represent motion, as well as use of "word" and "thought bubbles" to show a character's inner and outer voices are understood by children in Western cultures as early as age three (Hubbard, 1989).

Word Bubbles

In Brian's writing about his trip with his parents to New York City, he was excited to stay in a hotel. (Translation: *It was night time. We found a motel to stay in. I watched* Star Trek: The Next Generation.) In order to recreate the scene, he relies on both pictures and words. And it is important to him to capture the words out of his mother's mouth. For this, he effectively relies on the "word bubble," a convention he has seen in comic books (see Figure 5.4). "You're going to get brain rot," warns Brian's mother as he watches *Star Trek.* Brian's example also shows his willingness to adapt as well as borrow conventions from his environment. Because he wants to show the direction of her words, he writes the letters from right to left, as if they are emerging from her mouth.

FIGURE 5.4
Brian's trip to NYC

Angela uses word bubbles to add dimension to her drawing of the day she lost her tooth down the bathroom sink drain (see Figure 5.5). "Oops," Angela's mother says, as a horrified Angela screams, "Oh, no!" Even this small example shows the subtlety of Angela's understanding of convention: her mother's reaction is clearly not as emotional as Angela's, with the exclamation mark added for emphasis.

Action Lines

The use of action lines is another convention many children use early in their writing development to show motion and movement. In Western societies, movement of figures is frequently accentuated by lines, or sometimes a blur, even though real movement doesn't produce these effects. This is especially evident in cartoons, which are a daily part of children's environment in television, book illustrations, newspapers, and computer games.

Tatyana often writes about her difficulties with her bossy her older sister. Her story about her plans for revenge becomes more dramatic with the "action lines" that show her jumping up to "smack" her sister: "I want to give my sister a knuckle sandwich" (see Figure 5.6).

FIGURE 5.5
Angela loses her tooth

FIGURE 5.6
Tatyana gives her sister a "knuckle sandwich."

Key Points for Helping Children Learn about Conventions: Building on Teachable Moments

67

Key Points
for Helping
Children
Learn about
Conventions

Educators who use a developmental lens for working with their young writers keep foremost in their minds that learning conventions in writing is not different from other aspects of written language acquisition. Children are always learning to write within a cultural context. We can invite even very young children to have conversations about how a particular mark of punctuation or convention can be an aid to a writer.

In Lisa Cleaveland's first-grade class, students' interest in the use of ellipses in books sparked a classroom discussion about how writers can use punctuation in interesting ways. One student, Caleb, had "borrowed" this punctuation in his story about riding a roller coaster. The following excerpt from their class discussion illustrates the depth of children's thinking:

Lisa Cleaveland: How did it go with the roller coaster? What did you say on that page with the ellipsis?

Caleb: "But . . . I threw up."

Lisa: Yeah, it said something like, "We had fun on the roller coaster," and the next page said, "But . . ." and the next page said, "I threw up." So you kind of left us hanging when you said, "But . . ." You know, we *thought* you were going to say, "But . . . it wasn't that fast" or "I'm so cool it didn't scare me." But instead you were like, "But . . . I threw up." [laughter in the room]

Anna: It's like a guy hanging off a cliff.

Lisa: *It's like a guy hanging off a cliff.* I like that. Explain that. Tell us more.

Anna: It's like a guy hanging off a cliff and then everything freezes.

Lisa: Because that ellipsis is kind of leaving you hanging there, like "What's going to come next?"

Anna: Yeah, like he's thinking, "Am I going to fall off or stay on the cliff?"

Lisa: It's kind of got you in the middle, right? Like you're thinking it could go either way . . . You don't know where the text is going to go. I like that, Anna. (Katie Wood Ray, 2006, p. 10)

This discussion shows what is possible as children grapple with how to use conventions as tools for their writing. We can listen closely to their understandings and build from there.

Teaching Conventions

Specific minilessons to focus on the use of a variety of conventions can also help nudge children forward in their writing development. For example, it is very helpful to encourage children to listen as they read back their stories; dips in voice signal the need for a period; a lilt up at the end of a sentence often notes the need for a question mark.

In Andie Cunningham's kindergarten classroom, she often uses her own writing as a starting point for the class writing workshop. This morning, her minilesson is on writing with detail:

"Take a look. I have a funny story to tell." Andie points to the easel with a drawing of a dog and a large statue.

"I was out walking with Alysa, my daughter, and our dog, Bandit. I drew Bandit, see, grey with two dark circles around her eyes. And there was a big statue, and Bandit saw it and barked and barked. We laughed so hard, because Bandit never barks like that. But something made her bark. I drew those dark circles around her eyes, because that's an important detail. But I want to show her barking. How can I make that?"

Colton suggests, "You could make a line."

"Yeah, a line!" Kenzie agrees. "You should show Bandit's scared. You could put lines by her feet to show she's scared and movin' her feet around."

"Great idea! I'll add that suggestion. How can I show Bandit barking?"

Leonella softly suggests, "You could make like circles around."

"Oh, like a voice bubble? To show it's coming out of his mouth? OK, Oh, Ollie, you have another suggestion to go with that?"

"Uh huh," Ollie nods. "You could put the word 'bark' inside the circle."

"Oh, I love that idea! Help me show the letters that we need to write 'bark.'"

Together, the class sounds out *bark* and guides Andie to write "BRC" in a word bubble coming out of Bandit's mouth.

Andie looks at her writing with satisfaction. "That shows what I wanted. So, now, in your writing today, add your details. What's important in your writing? If

---

Key Points for Helping Children Learn about Conventions

1. Respect children's abilities to understand, use, and invent conventions. Build on their knowledge through individual and classroom discussions.
2. Encourage children to pay attention to the print (and other) media around them.
3. Create short focused lessons that show how conventions help the writer and reader, as appropriate.

you want to see how I finish this, stick around. Or go get your writing journals. Happy writing!"

Andie's minilesson helps put conventions in their proper perspective: interesting tools for writers to make their meaning more clear.

One of the exciting benefits of including a close look at conventions when discussing writing development is the chance to rediscover the ways that children are reading their literate worlds. It also opens up early childhood educators to the possibilities of a fascinating aspect of the written word that is largely taught as "correction" rather than "discovery." The world is full of fascinating writing that is enhanced by the range of conventions that help carry the messages. Filling our classrooms with models and rich discussions can bring new energy and life as well as new understanding to the teaching of writing.

Language to Language
Special Considerations for Working with Multilingual Writers

I sit in a small circle with several five-year-old children, as they pore through writing journals to share pieces that are ready for publication on the writing wall. The children have created a thoughtful process for inviting two mostly silent friends into the conversation about writing. One of those students, Mariaevelyn, rarely ventures words even in her native Spanish. The other, Lyuba, smiles her way through the day, just now beginning to mouth a word or two of either Russian or English.

Nonetheless, they are actively participating in the group conference. As Alma, David, and Tonia share their writing, they pass their journals over to Mariaevelyn and Lyuba. Each of these girls, in turn, ponders the page, then points to a section of the journal with a detail that she likes.

"Oh, you like the words?" Alma asks, as she follows Lyuba's pointed finger.

Lyuba nods.

Mariaevelyn likes the big yellow sun, and points to the upper right-hand corner. "I like the sun part, too," Alma confirms. "And I can make a rainbow."

Community. One of the intangibles that makes a classroom work and helps welcome all learners into the daily work. As children with many diverse backgrounds, cultures, and languages come together into learning environments from preschool on, it is vital that each person initiates actions that will invite each other's voices into the mix.

Many classrooms today are a stunning mix of background experiences, expert knowledge, languages, and cultures. Creating a literate classroom environment that nurtures the writing development of English language learners (ELL) requires more than a series of skills to learn or academics to master. Classrooms should be dedicated to building on children's knowledge, experience, and needs, and also to assisting in acquiring shared knowledge and understandings about what literacy is and how it can be a gift for communicating and learning.

Throughout this book, I have included examples and stories of the writing development of diverse learners, including those who are English language learners. They are part of the learning communities in the many classrooms in which I have worked and collected data; their learning is not isolated from other children in their classrooms. This chapter, though, will have a more directed focus on "best practice" for nurturing writing development with children who are learning English in addition to their first languages.

The majority of research that focuses on children's writing is based on native English-speaking children. But there is beginning to be more specific study of young English language learners as they develop as writers. In her recent book *When English Language Learners Write* (2006), Katharine Samway concludes that "the most current research shows that nonnative English speaking children are capable of much more than is generally expected of them" (p. 22).

Young English Language Learners' Awareness of Print

As we discussed in Chapter 2, young children across different languages and cultures reveal an awareness of the particular features of their native written language. Fouad's Arabic writing, for example, has lots of dots and squiggles, which he reads back in Arabic; Bao Jun's Chinese writing shows logographic characteristics. Both children also make shapes that represent the English alphabet that they see around them. Even very early "scribble writing" such as Cecilia's is reflective of cursive English.

73

Young
English
Language
Learners'
Awareness
of Print

Just as bilingual children immersed in dual languages sort out the two languages, creating hypotheses about how to speak both, young English language learners actively figure out the way written language works in the first and second languages. Katharine Samway (2006) stresses that a careful review of literature points to the need for English language learners to have access to what she calls "the creative construction principle" to allow their writing to emerge. In other words, children need the chance to explore and actively figure out the ways that written language works in different situations, continually trying out their hypotheses. Another researcher of bilingual developing writers, Emilia Ferreiro (1980) advises, "Children have shown us that they need to reconstruct the written system in order to make it their own. Let us allow them the time and the opportunities for such a tremendous task" (p. 56).

Five-year-old Song was allowed both time and opportunities in her kindergarten classroom. She entered school in the fall speaking a few words, phrases, and English expressions. Hmong is her first language and the language that her family speaks at home, although her family has English language skills strong enough that they do not need translators at conferences. Since there are no other Hmong speakers in the class, nor ethnic Hmong aides or translators at the school, English is what Emily used to communicate with her friends at school. She was by no means silent, though often quiet. She relied on gestures, pictures, and simple phrases and sentences in English to get her meaning across.

Her literacy grew steadily over the school year. In the fall, she drew many pictures and made a gradual transition to adding letters to go with them. She also copied letters from the English and Spanish words she saw in the classroom environment. By May, she began to use letters to represent sounds. In her drawing of water, she used an *r* for the /r/ sound. And on the very same page (see Figure 6.1), she used a string of Chinese characters, which she told us was the kind of writing her parents do. Her growing literacy in two languages seemed to help shore up her confidence to share her "at home" writing with us in school. In June, she was experimenting with exclamation marks, voice bubbles, and spaces between words, and created several books of her writing to share with friends. Her classroom environment allowed her the time and space to be an active and creative written language user.

FIGURE 6.1

Song's Chinese characters

Song is not an exception. English language learners can write before orally mastering the English language (Edelsky, 1982; Hudleson, 1989; Taylor, 2000; Samway, 2006). Just like native-speaking children, they can write before they are able to read and can use drawing to explore their ideas and thinking.

Russian-speaking Kostya came to kindergarten speaking no English, but was very willing to use gesture and facial expression to communicate with adults and other children in the room. He usually looked very serious when he opened his writing journal, and when he sat down to write it was with intention. One morning, his story was about the truck that his father drives (see Figure 6.2). Like all good writers, Kostya used detail in his piece, from the lug nuts in the tires, to the steering wheel, to the exhaust coming out of the pipe at the rear of the vehicle. He even included the arms of the passengers dangling out of the windows. When asked, Kostya explained his drawing (in Russian), but knowing I could not understand, supplemented his verbal explanation with pointing, movement, and gesture. Our "conversation" helped his language development, as I continued to guess his meaning, supplying English words for car (he shook his head no), and bus (no again, with a smile this time). But I was rewarded with an emphatic "Yes!" when I offered, "Truck?"

"Yes, truck!" he repeated, which drew in his neighbors, Luis and Tony, to our conversation sparked by Kostya's drawing.

Researchers Ernst and Richard (1995) in their investigation of the role of talk in developing English language learners' literacy, found that talk was indeed an important influence on the students' developing fluency in English, both oral and written. Using writing and drawing as conversation starters helps children share interest and their own stories in response to each other's (Hubbard, 1985).

FIGURE 6.2

Kostya's truck

KOSTYA

Name: _____ date: _____

The Role of Native Languages in Writing Development

75

The Role
of Native
Languages
in Writing
Development

Bilingual programs have an obvious advantage. Research has shown that children who gain literacy in their first language do not need to relearn these skills. English language learners who learn to read in their native language do not need to be taught to read in English; they simply transfer the skill to their second language. The same holds true for writing (Freeman & Freeman, 2003; Schecter & Bayley, 2002).

In diverse schools with many languages spoken, bilingual programs for every language are not feasible. But it is beneficial whenever possible to find native speakers to talk and write with young children.

Kindergartner Alma wrote a complex story one day, in pictures. She began to write out sounds to label the story. *Cat* and *twins* were the two English words that stood out in her story, and in an attempt to help her, a classroom helper dictated letters to her. These were not words she could read back, so she turned from this story in frustration.

But when Alma was encouraged to tell her story in Spanish to our bilingual classroom aide, the words poured out of her, a story of a girl who had a twin who died in Mexico. Now, the other twin thinks of her. *(Una nina tiene una gemala que una vez se murio. Ahorra la gemela esta pensando en ella. Ella esta en el cemetaria.)* And Alma made the leap of sounding out words in Spanish to write her story, "*merta*" (*muerta*). (See Figure 6.3.)

FIGURE 6.3

Alma's twin story

Marina, a five-year-old Russian speaker appreciated every chance she had to speak with Luba, the Russian aide and translator at the school. On her own, Marina created a little book in writing workshop with some writing in English and a few Cyrillic letters as well, with words like "CPMAS" for "Christmas." And she felt comfortable taking the risk of speaking to me and others with a few words of English.

Her writing rose to new heights, though, when Christina, a visiting teacher, came to the classroom for the day. When Marina discovered that Christina could read and write Russian, this quiet girl became a chatterbox. Because Luba is the school's only Russian aide, her visits are quite brief; what a gift to have Christina for the entire morning! Marina wrote the story of her mom drying the clothes out in the sun. She wrote *sun* in English, using one set of symbols: (*CAOA*) and *conyue, sun* in Russian, written using Cyrillic. *Clothes* and *drying the clothes* are both written in Russian, too, using invented spelling (see Figure 6.4).

Because Christina was able to talk and write with Marina in both languages, Marina was encouraged to write and talk in Russian and English as well.

Marina was not the only student to benefit from Christina's presence. Lyuba simply beamed as she sat with Christina. She wrote *SN* for *sun* in English, then told her the Russian words for house (*dom*) and flower (*ubemon*; see Figure 6.5). This is a huge leap for Lyuba, as she seldom speaks a word, in any language.

The next morning, we saw that Marina's work with Christina had really sparked a leap in her willingness to take risks in her writing, experimenting with both Russian and English in different genres. In writing workshop, she chose to mimic the sign-in routine in the classroom, which is often a survey or question of some kind.

Marina copied the letters to write, "Do you like ice cream?" Underneath these words she wrote her little brother's name, Nika, using the letters *NuKA,* a combination of the letter used for English (*N*) and Russian (*uKA*). Beneath it she wrote a string of letters from the Cyrillic alphabet that can be sounded out as "*pazgravit*" or "to greet" (see Figure 6.6).

Another student in the same class, Bennie, also made strides in his writing in the spring when he read his journal and explained his drawings in Cantonese when his mother came for a conference. Though he was now speaking more in English in class than he had earlier in the year, and would tell about his writing in English phrases and gestures, we never got to hear such complete thoughts about his writing as we did through that conference with his parents.

FIGURE 6.4
Marina's mom drying clothes

FIGURE 6.5
Lyuba's story

FIGURE 6.6
Marina's Cyrillic sign-in sheet

Like Marina, Bennie made a big leap in his writing after this conference in his native language. The same week, he shared two pieces of writing with me: the first was a kind of picture story about spiders, birds, and his brother and sister (Figure 6.7). His English letters wrote out his Cantonese name, Ming, as well as Bennie. He also included his brother's English name, Alex, as well as a row of letters. But on the same day, he also wrote a story in Chinese logographs—a skill we had never seen him use in class before (Figure 6.8). At the end of the day, I saw him tuck this writing into his jacket pocket to bring home and share with his parents.

Stories like these provide additional support for the research that shows that English language learners can write in both their home and nonnative languages without becoming confused. In a fascinating year-long ethnography, Edelsky and Jilbert (1985) found that children learned both Spanish and English simultaneously without confusion and were able to differentiate between the two writing systems. In their Spanish invented spellings, the children used tildes (~) and never used the letter *k,* which is used in Spanish only for foreign words. In any of their writing they read back in English, there were no tildes and they did include the letter *k.*

In a review of the literature, Samway (2006) found that writing processes for young children are very similar across languages. Children whose native language is logographic, such as Chinese and Korean, rather than alphabetic, like English or Spanish, invent spellings and writing symbols (Chi, 1988). Even when children are learning two very different written language systems, they draw on their knowledge of their native language as well as their growing understanding of English, testing out hypotheses just as they do in their oral language (Edelsky & Jilbert, 1985).

FIGURE 6.7

Bennie's picture story

FIGURE 6.8

Bennie's Chinese writing

What about Children in the Silent Period?

If you have a new English language learner in your class who is not speaking, you are not alone. According to language researcher Stephen Krashen (1985), most new learners of English will go through a "silent period," where they are unwilling or unable to communicate orally, even though they understand much of what is going on around them. They are not comfortable speaking in the new language, because it is difficult for them to express their thoughts orally. Children in this silent period should not be forced to speak before they are ready. They need time to listen to others talk, digest what they hear, and observe their fellow classmates' interactions with each other. Remaining silent doesn't mean they are not learning the language.

It is easy to understand the concept of the "silent period" if you look at the language learning of babies. Babies in any culture can understand far more than they express. In a class of children who speak many languages other than English at home, you will often have children in the silent period—they are learning many English words, ideas, and idioms, but they are not comfortable speaking as part of the group or individually.

The length of the silent period can vary greatly for students in classrooms, from a few days to a year, simply because their experience with language, their personalities, and their emotions around learning a new language can vary so greatly. When children are silent in the dominant classroom language, it can be hard to assess their progress in acquiring English.

The silent period at any age can last many months—even children who understand a tremendous number of words and concepts are overwhelmed at the thought of trying to speak in the language. But if we convey through our verbal and non-verbal cues that we want to communicate and trust the communication will come, children will eventually speak. Classrooms that are engaging, nonthreatening, and honor a child's native language and culture can help each student's motivation, risk taking, and ability to learn.

Andie Cunningham and I created a list of suggestions for conferring with English language learners (2006). We base these suggestions on what has worked for us, and encourage you to add to this list as you discover other strategies.

When conferring with English language learners in our classroom, we use these strategies to communicate verbally and nonverbally:

- We ask questions that allow the child to respond with nods of "yes" or "no." These prompts include guesses of what the child is drawing or about the marks they are making on the page (i.e., "Is that your mother?" "Is this writing in Russian?" "In English?")

- We accept as response facial expressions like smiles. Nonverbal cues from children in conferences include establishing eye contact, flipping through pages of writing for us, pointing to specific pictures or letters, or grabbing our hands to touch the page or help the child draw a letter.

- We share a word or two in the child's language. This might be the Spanish word for "butterfly" if we are studying butterflies in science, or the Russian word for "mother" if we think the child has drawn a picture of their mother. Because there are so many different first languages in our classroom, we rely on bilingual dictionaries and suggestions from native language speakers. If the alphabet is the same as the English alphabet, simple Web translators can be helpful ("Babblefish" at www.babblefish.com and "Free Translation" at www.freetranslation.com). These are only useful for basic literal translations, but children appreciate the attempt. (These websites will also translate several sentences into another written language such as Vietnamese, Russian, or Chinese, which can be helpful for brief notes to parents.)

- We ask the child to teach us words in their language. They usually know the word "Chinese" or "Spanish" when you ask how to say something like "pencil" or "book" in their language.

- Many children draw pictures of their families. When this occurs, we point to each figure and ask if this is the mother, or sister, or brother, and if they nod, we ask the name of the family member. The first words of children in the silent period are often related to family.

- Watch the child on the playground. If there is no verbal communication in the classroom, there are often early words around play.

- We ask children to mime the action of what they are trying to convey using their bodies to communicate.

- Ask the child to draw a picture of what they are trying to tell you.

Sometimes we underestimate the power of friendship and community in language learning. Lyuba taught me an important lesson one day as I was conferring with her about her writing, as the following excerpt from my field notes show:

> Lyuba is a wonder. She takes in the world around her with smiles and enthusiasm, though she is still in the "silent period" for English. Today for the first time she accepted Andie's invitation to place a card in the calendar chart. Her confidence is growing daily. As a native Russian speaker, she faces many challenges in a kindergarten with only one other Russian speaker. But she turns with enthusiasm to her writing projects. I ask her questions, and she always answers me with conviction, nodding either yes or no. Her drawing is definitely of a mountain, with her two sisters. The "m" seems to represent the mound for mountain. But I am also intrigued by the string of letters—the alphabet—that runs under her drawing [see Figure 6.9].
>
> I ask her if the writing tells the story of her picture. Yes, she nods.
>
> "Is it in Russian?"
>
> An unmistakable *no* head shake (as in, *Are you crazy?*)
>
> "In English then?"
>
> A nod and a smile.

FIGURE 6.9

Lyuba's "English writing"

Lyuba also showed me how helpful it is to have another child present when I have a writing conference with her. We were able to communicate: She would smile and tell me whether I guessed right, with a head nod or shake and a big smile. But one day, she ran and brought her friend Alma to our writing conference. Though Alma's first language was Spanish and she spoke no Russian, she was a wonderful translator for her special friend. Because they knew each other so well, Alma was able to help Lyuba get her meaning across to me and others in the classroom, adding her own gestures, pictures, and giggles to Lyuba's.

These two instances show the importance of an environment that encourages genuine communication, by whatever means will work. Children need access to caring adults who will persevere to make sense of what each child is trying to share, and they need to be able to rely on each other as part of a learning community. Rather than a teacher sitting at a desk focused on individual learning tasks, a workshop

Key Points for Nurturing English Language Learners' Writing Development

81

The
Importance of
Community
and
Environment

1. Look at each child as an individual. All writers are unique and their writing development will reflect those idiosyncrasies. Get to know the children with whom you work, their interests and their writing processes.

2. Encourage children to write and draw their stories right from the beginning, before they have mastered oral English.

3. Create opportunities for sharing writing with other adults in the classroom and among the young writers themselves.

4. Allow children the time and space they need to test out their hypotheses about written language.

5. Provide as many opportunities as possible in children's first language.

6. Surround children with print in a range of languages and alphabet systems. (See the resources below.)

atmosphere encourages children to determine what tools, peers, and mentors will aid them in their quest to make meaning.

Alphabet Books and Beyond: Picture Books for Young English Language Learners. Five-year-old Bao Jun lived two-thirds of her young life in China, then moved to Portland, Oregon. On the first day of kindergarten, her mother told me, "You say, she understand. Sometime she not know word to tell." Bao Jun used her new English in her writing and speaking, cautiously at first. In late September, in her "expert painting," she used watercolors to paint Chinese characters and tell us, "I am an expert at my Chinese writing." To build on her expert knowledge and share that expertise with the class, I bought the book *At the Beach* by Huy Youn Lee. In this book, Xiao Ming and his mother go to the beach, where Xiao Ming likes to draw Chinese figures in the sand with a stick. On each double page of the book, a Chinese character is introduced. Bao Jun's eyes lit up when she recognized the symbols in the picture book, and she soon began to write in both Chinese logography and in English during writing workshop.

Young English language learners benefit from seeing different alphabet books, scripts, and logograph-based writing systems as part of their classroom library. While it has become fairly easy to find good bilingual alphabet books for Spanish speakers, other languages can present more of a challenge. The following is a beginning recommended list of books that will invite young writers to delight in the variety of languages and scripts from their own home language and those of their classmates.

Ada, Alma Flor 1997. *Gathering the sun: An alphabet in Spanish and English.* Illus. by Simon Silva. New York: HarperCollins. In this stunning bilingual alphabet book, Alma Flor Ada matches each letter with a Spanish word (for example, "Arboles" for "A") and adds a poem in both Spanish and English that describes how the plant, fruit, vegetable, person, or feeling functions in the lives of these workers. The poems are short and simple, but lyrical and match the brilliance of the illustrations. The focus on the daily life of the migrant farm worker makes it a great text for older children as well.

Fedor, Jane. 1995. *Table, chair, bear: A book in many languages. English, Korean, French, Arabic, Vietnamese, Japanese, Portuguese, Lao, Spanish, Chinese, Tagalog, Cambodian, Navaho.* Boston, MA: Ticknor/Houghton. This book is neither a storybook nor an alphabet book, but does provide a chance to explore twelve different languages. A simple naming scheme pairs everyday objects with labels. The English word is set at the top of the page in bold lowercase letters while a list running down the side of the cleancut page depicts the word in each original language with phonetic pronunciation added. A final double-page spread depicts a child's room containing all the previously named items, and the author's note explains the phonetic sounds and symbols.

Heide, Florence Parry, & Judith Heide Gilliland. 1990. *The day of Ahmed's secret.* Illus. by Ted Lewis. New York: Lothrop Books. Readers follow Ahmed through a day in the streets of Cairo as he delivers canisters of cooking gas. Beautifully illustrated in watercolor, the book is told in Ahmed's voice and through his eyes as he shares his daily routine and enjoyment of his family life. His secret is revealed on the last page of the book, when he demonstrates to his family that he has learned to write his name in Arabic script.

Hill, Margaret Bateson. 2005. *Masha and the firebird.* Illus. by Anne Wilson. London, U.K.: Evans Publishing Group. This Russian tale is a blending of the Firebird legend and other traditional folktales. Masha helps support her family by selling her brilliantly painted eggs. In the forest, she meets the Firebird, who asks her to hide her eggs by painting beautiful designs on them. When Masha learns that Baba Yaga has stolen one egg, she travels to the witch's house, which burns in a dramatic, mystical battle, with a new Firebird emerging from the ashes. The illustrations are rich and vivid, appealing to the children I have shared it with. It is one of the few bilingual Russian/English texts I have found with stories that appeal to very young children.

Lee, Huy Youn. 1998. *At the beach.* New York: Henry Holt. As Xiao Ming walks along the beach with his mother, she teaches him several Chinese characters and explains how they show what they represent. Readers learn along with Xiao Ming in this first of a series of books that teach different Chinese symbols and explain their derivation. Equally fine are Lee's other books, *In the Park* and *In the Snow.* (Note: Mandarin pronunciation guides are also provided. Cantonese speakers will recognize the characters but pronounce each differently than the text guides.)

Mado, Michio. 1998. *The magic pocket.* Illus. by Mitsumasa Anno. Translated by the Empress Michiko of Japan. English and Japanese. Margaret McElderry Books. This simple book, with bright images, is sparely presented, yet compelling. Simple images convey childhood experiences such as breaking a cookie in your pocket, walking under an umbrella, or listening to the sounds of musical instruments. Both the original Japanese and the English translations are included.

Recorvits, Helen. 2003. *My name is Yoon.* Illus. by Gabi Swiatkowska. New York: Frances Foster Books. Yoon is the narrator of this story of a young Korean immigrant. Yoon's name means Shining Wisdom, and when she writes it in Korean, it looks happy, "like dancing figures." Her father teaches her to write Yoon in English, and she is not pleased with the way the writing looks on the page, even though her father stresses it still means "shining wisdom." Though there is little Korean writing in the text, the book does a good job of exploring Yoon's mixed emotions about the differences emotionally in writing in two different languages.

Rumford, James. 2001. *Traveling man: The journey of Ibn Battuta, 1325–1354*. Boston, MA: Houghton Mifflin. Ibn Battuta was a fourteenth-century explorer who recorded his journey from Morocco to China, and from Russia to the shores of Tanzania (seventy thousand miles in all). James Rumsford retells and illustrates Ibn Battuta's story. While the story itself might be more geared to older children, the beautiful Arabic calligraphy will entice young readers. The calligraphy flows across colorful maps and bright images of the ancient world.

Rumford, James. 2000. *Seeker of knowledge: The man who deciphered Egyptian hieroglyphs*. Boston, MA: Houghton Mifflin. Jean-Francois Champollion became fascinated with Egyptian hieroglyphs when he saw the writing on Egyptian treasures when he was seven years old. This book chronicles his search to decipher the ancient writings. The text is richly illustrated with watercolors and with the hieroglyphs themselves. Each hieroglyph is translated both as a picture and what it came to mean. For example, an unblinking crocodile creates the word "trouble." *Seeker of Knowledge* is a wonderful conversation-starter to pique interest in pictographs and a range of writing systems.

Stories
Writing, Talking, and Listening to Develop Language and Literacy Skills

One day when Adi Rule was nearly five years old, she passed her mother, Becky, a piece of paper with the following writing:

NASHNL-NOOSPAPR	National Newspaper
THISWKAND	This weekend
AT THE RULE	at the Rules'
BABDUCK	baby ducks
GRODBIGR	growed bigger.

Becky was thrilled with her daughter's "newspaper article" and couldn't resist asking her one question: "What else happened?" A few minutes later, Adi returned with a second news item:

OSOTHISWKAND	Also this weekend
THERULES WENT	the Rules went
TOHRMIT	to Hermit
ILEND	Island.

Reported in *Write from the Start* by Donald Graves and Virginia Stuart, 1985, p. 214.

Adi is hard at work, making sense of her world and the events around her. And she is using her writing to help her select and organize the details of her experience into a story. Stories are one of the most enriching contexts for the development of language, both spoken and written.

The Role of Story

Around three or so years of age, a child takes another great leap in development, a leap that makes her a "different" child while still remaining herself . . . Finally a child can tell herself the story of the events and experiences that happen to her. She can now weave together an autobiographical narrative.

—Daniel Stern

The ability to frame experiences into a narrative—into a *story*—marks a huge developmental leap in language acquisition. The number of words a child knows and understands may not have changed, but her ability to create a story from a flow of sequences helps the child interpret the events into a meaningful experience. As child psychologist Daniel Stern (1990) concludes, "Because story making (and story telling) is common to all cultures, and an expected developmental landmark for all children, we now think of story making as a universal human capacity" (p. 132).

Stories create organization for the developing child's mind. He can draw from past memories and experiences and make connections to what is occurring in the present. He can mix together events and memories that happened at different times and places and can also mix in imaginary or "pretend" elements (Stern, 1990). He is creating a structure with a beginning, middle, and end, telling that plot line first to himself, and then to an audience.

Written stories as well as oral stories are an integral part of the development of a child in a literate culture. Listening to stories has proven to be the most helpful preparation for the acquisition of literacy. Long before children can read themselves, children who listen to stories are already beginning to gain experience in the organization of written language and its characteristic rhythms and structures (Heath 1982; Wells, 1986).

While the importance of reading aloud to children has been well established, less attention is typically paid to the role that writing stories and reading them aloud can play.

Children Writing
Stories—Another Developmental Leap

During the preschool and early school years, children begin to tell stories based on their experiences, selecting significant events and organizing them into plots with beginnings, middles, and ends (Leondar, 1977; Applebee, 1978; Dyson, 1988). They use talk, drawing, and writing to organize and make sense of their experiences. Children's drawings are often very important as elements of their writing, as discussed in Chapter 3. Drawing is important for our earliest writers, as researcher Anne Haas Dyson notes, "because it helps children plan and organize their dictated or written text" (Dyson, 1988, p. 26;). Children begin with simple labeling of their drawings, then begin to use both drawings and written symbols to expand and organize events in their lives on paper.

Molly's drawing of her loose tooth (Figure 7.1) sparks her writing: "I have a loose tooth," with the accompanying diagram and arrow "right here." This is the beginning of moving into telling the story of that loose tooth. Notice how Steven also uses his drawing as a spark for creating a beginning narrative of his "bad day" (Figure 7.2): "I'm having a bad day. I got up to play my Nintendo. But my Mom would not let me play."

Steven is at a critical point where he can make a transition into "storying" (Wells, 1986) or creating an effective sequence of events through writing. Gordon Wells concludes in his landmark Bristol Study research that "it is not that young children lack stories to tell or write, it is rather that some lack familiarity with the way in which stories are constructed and given expression in writing" (1986, p. 202).

FIGURE 7.1

Molly's loose tooth

FIGURE 7.2

Steven's bad day

FIGURE 7.3

Luke's narrative

Some students may make this leap on their own, through being in an environment rich with stories and the opportunity to write. Luke wrote this story over three days in his classroom writing journal (see Figure 7.3). He shows his understanding of "beginning, middle, and end" very clearly in his three-page story: "This is a duck"; "A duck is swimming"; and "And the duck lived happily ever after." A story such as this shows Luke's understanding of sequencing the events he wants to share. It is also clear that he has an understanding of the differences in language use for written texts, with his use of the convention "happily ever after" for his tale.

Expectations for helping children frame narratives should not be left to chance. Besides whole-class opportunities to write, children also benefit from one-on-one conversations around their writing and drawing, which help them frame their experiences into written stories.

Alma's writing began to bloom from simple labeling such as a drawing of a butterfly with the letter *b,* or a drawing of a horse with the label *RS* for *horse* in May when her teacher Andie Cunningham made time to talk with her about the story she wanted to tell. Alma began with a little slip of paper with a stick figure of herself (labeled "Me yelling 'Mom'"). (See Figure 7.4.)

FIGURE 7.4

Alma's story beginning and narrative

when I screamed Mom.

"What's happening here?" Andie asked.

"That's when I screamed for Mom," Alma explained.

Andie drew out the details of the event with Alma, which helped her develop her idea into a five-page story, using the conventions of letters and voice bubbles. Using questions like "What happened next?" and "How can you put that on paper? What sounds do you hear?" helped Alma complete her story of riding her scooter, crashing, falling and hurting herself, calling for Mom, then concluding by telling her mother the sad saga on the last page: "Wt hapnd [*What happened*]?" her mother asks. "I fl [*I fell*]," Alma tells her. (Refer back to Figure 7.4 for the rest of the story.) Story writing experiences like this provide a real purpose for children to extend control over language. "For all children, stories continue to provide the most enriching contexts for the development of language, both spoken and written" (Wells, 1986, p. 203).

Caregivers and early childhood educators can also tap into children's storying abilities by creating opportunities for them to organize events from their lives into sequences. This is best accomplished by looking closely at what children already know and building from that knowledge. Primary teacher Jenny Francis wanted to help all her students understand the importance of sequencing events. She began by asking them to think of something they knew how to do. Children volunteered experiences such as making a cake, planting flowers, riding a bike, or playing kickball.

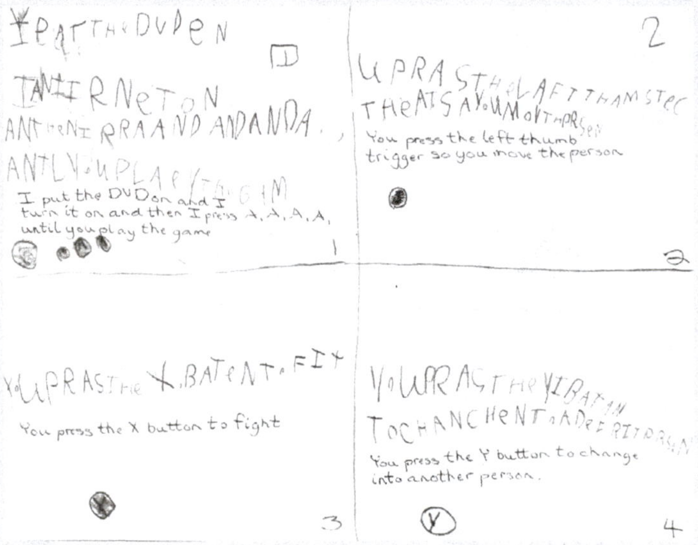

Jenny took a large sheet of paper and folded it into four squares. "Devon, if you wanted to explain how to play your video game in steps in each of these squares, what could you say?"

Devon explained the sequence in the following four steps (Figure 7.5):

FIGURE 7.5

Devon's Nintendo sequence

1. I put the DVD on and I turn it on and I press A,A,A,A until you play the game.

2. You press the left thumb trigger so you move the person.

3. You press the X button to fight.

4. You press the Y button to change into another person.

All the children in Jenny's class were able to complete this sequencing "how to" through their own life experiences, no matter what their writing proficiency. Some children relied more on pictures than words, but each child was able to create a sequenced plot based on their own expertise.

Henry's pictures show the nuance that his words can't yet describe. In order to watch TV, there are four steps in Henry's plot line:

1. First sit on couch
2. Then you get the remote and turn the TV on.
3. Then you choose the channel.
4. Then you watch it.

Notice that the figure preparing to watch TV is sitting straight up until the final panel, where he sinks back into a relaxing pose to watch TV! (See Figure 7.6.)

FIGURE 7.6

Henry's TV sequence

While Melanie's story of making a cake is all in the format of "I need . . . ," she is still using sequencing, from the beginning of the process: "I need a bowl," and then flour, eggs, and, last, frosting. (See Figure 7.7.)

Lydia uses both words and pictures to describe a ballet leap. (See Figure 7.8.) The positioning of her arms and legs in her pictures is crucial and matches her words:

1. Relax your legs and arms.
2. Spread your legs apart.
3. Arms apart and legs.
4. (no words, but a drawing of a figure in mid-air leap)

FIGURE 7.7

Melanie's cake sequence

FIGURE 7.8

Lydia's ballet leap sequence

Whole-class lessons on sequencing like Jenny's build from students' knowledge and help teachers both assess and instruct students in a strategy that naturally lends itself to storytelling and story writing. No prepared worksheet asking students to arrange figures, actions, or words, could fit so naturally into the curriculum and meet each student's needs.

Sharing Stories

Listening to stories read aloud at the age of two, three, or four—long before they can read themselves—children are already beginning to gain experience of the sustained meaning-making organization of written language and its characteristic rhythms and structures.

—Gordon Wells

When children have heard stories read aloud, reading and writing for themselves feels far more natural. The language and structure they have encountered through the pleasure of the storybook experience serves them well, building an important foundation.

Stories are also important "conversation starters" for collaborative talk. When adults and children share stories together, those stories are a wonderful starting point for children to continue to build on the experience on the page, connecting their own experiences and exploring their own world in the light of what has happened in the story. Adults play a vital role in validating the child's experiences and encouraging their extensions of the stories.

Children can work together to share their written stories and these, too, can be the basis for collaborative talk. When writers put words to paper, they are writing to an imagined audience. The audience might be themselves at another point in time; it might be a specific friend; it might be an anonymous group of readers they never meet. When we institute writing workshops with primary school–age writers, it's important to provide genuine audiences for their written work. Young children who write are no different than other authors; they need a chance to share their work through conferences and conversations.

Many kindergarten, first- and second-grade teachers struggle with a tension in their writing workshops: How do you introduce the notion of conferencing to young writers, many of whom do not yet "read"?

In order to try it out one morning, Andie Cunningham and I decide to introduce conferences with her five- and six-year-old authors by modeling with our own writing. Journals in hand, Andie and I sit in the circle before the twenty-three kindergartners at the end of writing workshop time. Andie explains that we will be reading what we wrote today to each other to have a conference. Andie reads her page to me and shows me her picture.

"Now, Ruth will tell me what she loves about my writing." I tell Andie how her drawing of her dog Bandit reminds me of my own childhood dog Spottie and how I love that she wrote about the way Bandit barked to get her attention. Next, I read my short text about seeing the moon this morning as I drove to school. Andie tells me what she loves about *my* writing: "I love that you noticed the same thing I did this morning! And I love the words you use to tell about what you saw in the sky."

The children listen as we talk about our writing in these brief conferences.

"Now, it's your turn." Andie pairs the children off, calling out, "Austin, you'll be partners with Nathaniel. Bianca, share your writing with Brooke." When all the children are in pairs, Andie asks them to share the writing they did today in writing workshop, and tell their partner what *they* love about the writing.

Fast forward two weeks. To start writing workshop time, Andie asks three children to show their writing to the class. Kenya shows the drawing he did of a picture frame, then the letters that he put on the paper. "So Kenya did his drawing first, then he did his writing."

Next, Taylor shares her picture. "I didn't write yet."

"So she could add more to it. That's what I do. Your journals are on the table. Go to work, writers."

As the children write, Andie and I circulate, holding individual conferences. After about fifteen minutes, Andie gives us the one-minute warning to finish up our writing, and we move to the sharing circle.

"Think back to when Ruth and I shared our writing and we told each other what we loved about it. Today you'll have time to do that with a friend. Kenya and Refugio, you'll be partners." Andie pairs the students until she reaches Austin S., who asks, "Can we make it maybe be three people today?"

"What do you think?" Andie asks the group.

A resounding "Yeah!" shifts the plans for the day. Andie quickly regroups the children into threes and helps them sit so they are in minicircles, and then the three-way conferences begin.

I am privileged to sit in on Carrie, Emely, and Lacey. Lacey begins.

She reads her piece, "Me and my mom walk our dog in the yard." She looks up at her conference group and says, "My dog died."

Emely: It's good you wrote about him. I love that you can remember him now.

Lacey: It makes me sad . . . [The three girls sit in silence for a moment. Then Lacey adds] And my Grandma died, too.

Emely: I'm so sorry about that.

Lacey: Now you read, Emely.

Emely [reads]: "I love my Grandma" [shows her picture to her audience]

Carrie: What do we love about Emely's?

These young children know how to follow the format of a writing conference, and they know it's fine to add verbally to what they have written, having genuine conversations about their stories. Our youngest writers need the chance for this authentic aspect of writing. They show they can learn from conferences in a range of formats: with their teacher, with a partner, with the whole class, and in small writing response groups.

As children progress through elementary school and beyond, they can continue to build on their oral and written language foundation. (See Appendix B for a list of recommended texts for facilitating writing development with children as they progress as writers through adolescence.) Principles that aid adults in nurturing oral language are also important guiding principles at all ages:

- Treat what the child has to say as worthy of careful attention.
- Try to understand what he or she means.
- Build from what the child says when you respond.

All teaching is about relationships with the children in our care, whether we work with toddlers, young children, or adolescents. Our young people need positive nurturing relationships with caring adults who are themselves readers and writers and who will foster children's interest and enjoyment in literacy. Young writers need opportunities to talk, tell stories, hear stories and write stories, using nonconventional forms such as invented spelling at first and, over time, learning to use conventional forms.

We need to lean in and listen closely to each individual child, adapting instruction to meet their needs, marveling at the miracle of their differences, nurturing them at all stages. Our students deserve our respect for their amazing capabilities and potential. As literacy researcher Donald Graves (2002) advises, "Focus on the writer, and the writing will come." When we concentrate our energies on raising writers to delight in the written word and the power of their stories, they come to see writing as a natural way to share what's going on in their minds and get support and feedback to extend their thinking.

As my young friend and fellow author Emma writes:

I love writing nice stories so I can get compliments. I like people clapping for my stories. I love, love, love good stories like my own. I love to share my ideas for the world to see what they think about them. P.S. Writing is lots of fun!

The End

Name EMMA

I love writing nice storie so I
can git compemints! I like peopel
claping for my stories, I love
love love good stories like Myown.
I love to share my ideyes for the
world to see wat they think
about them. p.s. writing is lots of
un! the end

Developmental Progression in Invented Spelling

1. Random letters to represent meaning

"I just write 'em; I don't read 'em."

The first stage in invented spelling is when children put down strings of letters that are simply combinations of letters they know how to make, as Nicole did in Figure A.1

FIGURE A.1
Nicole's random letters

2. Labeling with beginning phonetic spelling

Most often initial consonants, then initial and ending, but sometimes the letters that a child knows from her own name or from letters with clear sound-symbol correspondence (*I*, *S*, *R*). (See Figures A.2 and A.3.)

Brooke

Name:_____date:_____

FIGURE A.2
Brooke's "ladybug"

101

Name: BIANCA   date:_____

FIGURE A.3
Bianca's "sun"

3. Growing sound-symbol correspondence

A combination of how words sound and how words look. In this stage, children incorporate more use of vowels. (See Figure A.4.)

FIGURE A.4
Amelia's "butterfly"

FIGURE A.5
Lacey's "me and my dog walking in the park"

4. Moving toward convention: Further refinement

Use of multistrategies for spelling. Further refinement where letters represent more sounds in words. Some words are invented, and others are remembered. (See Figure A.6.)

FIGURE A.6
Chris' "Chicks like to stay warm. They grow new feathers"

Books to Support Writing Development for Children and Adolescents

Some of the best resources are written by teachers who work with children and adolescents every day in the classroom. The texts below are by teachers and writing coaches whose theoretical and practical advice comes from the real worlds of the students with whom they work.

Elementary Focus

Avery, Carol. 2002. *And with a light touch: Learning about reading, writing, and teaching with first graders.* Portsmouth, NH: Heinemann.

> Carol Avery writes with the practical knowledge of one who has been there. She generously shares the structures that can create a truly response-based classroom environment. With numerous student samples and stories from her writing workshop, Carol demonstrates how to nurture young writers. I especially appreciate the way she weaves authentic assessment into her explanations of teaching.

Buckner, Aimee. 2005. *Notebook know-how: Strategies for the writer's notebook.* Portland, ME: Stenhouse.

> *Notebook Know-How* provides readers with the tools for using a writer's notebook as part of writing instruction for children in grades three through eight. Aimee Buckner demonstrates how to introduce the notebook to students and how to help them continue to rely on it as a resource for their writing development, along with practical tips for teachers such as mini lessons and assessment strategies.

Hindley, Joanne. 1996. *In the company of children.* Portland, ME: Stenhouse.

> Third-grade teacher Joanne Hindley takes you into her classroom and tells the stories of the readers and writers within it. This is the book I use when working with preservice and inservice teachers, as it reads like a novel and is brimming with useful advice and strategies for teachers in setting up reading and writing workshops. This great guide is especially useful when gleaning suggestions for successful writing conferences with students.

Karelitz, Ellen Blackburn. 1993. *The author's chair and beyond.* Portsmouth, NH: Heinemann.

> Ellen Blackburn Karelitz brings her experiences teaching literacy to primary age children across the curriculum to this text. Ellen originally coined the term "the author's chair" early in the writing process movement. Her pioneer work shows the respect she holds for the young children with whom she works. Teachers

appreciate hearing the stories of the children in her classroom as they use writing to make meaning in the writing workshop, as well as the ways children write notes to Karelitz and each other and to document their understanding of concepts in math and science.

Ray, Katie Wood, & Lisa Cleaveland. 2004. *About the author: Writing workshop with our youngest writers.* Portsmouth, NH: Heinemann.

Ray, Katie Wood, & Lisa Cleaveland. 2006. *Study driven: A framework for planning units of study in the writing workshop.* Portsmouth, NH: Heinemann.

Both of these texts are highly recommended for working with "our youngest writers" and beyond. Rich with examples from Lisa Cleaveland's classroom, *About the Authors* explains with clarity and respect how to create writing workshops that honor what young children bring to using print to make meaning. In *Study Driven,* Ray details her method for using a mentor-texts approach to teaching writing. Ray shows how to set up a writing workshop using published texts that supports children's learning, leading to an understanding of the traits of good writing.

Secondary Focus

Atwell, Nancie. 1998. *In the middle: New understanding about writing, reading, and learning.* Portsmouth, NH: Heinemann.

In the Middle helped spark a revolution in literacy teaching with adolescents. Nancie Atwell brings readers into the world of young teens, honoring what they bring to their writing and reading attempts, their struggles, and successes. Based on student choice and thoughtful mentoring, Atwell's text is widely considered the classic handbook for organizing and teaching writing workshops in middle schools.

Christensen, Linda. 2000. *Reading, writing, and rising up: Teaching about social justice and the power of the written word.* Milwaukee, WI: Rethinking Schools.

Linda Christensen inspires her readers to follow her lead and create classroom writing communities that help students improve their writing academically and, at the same time, work to change the world through social action. This empowering text is written with grace and clarity. Christensen generously shares numerous strategies she has used in her classrooms, and unpacks lessons to show what works and how she changes curricula to meet the needs of her students.

Rief, Linda. 1992. *Seeking diversity: Language arts with adolescents.* Portsmouth, NH: Heinemann.

Linda Rief has been teaching writing and reading to adolescents for twenty years. Her experience with the subject matter and the students comes across in this practical text that tells the story of her writing with seventh- and eighth-grade students. Her chapters on assessment and use of portfolios are particularly useful. Teachers also love the wealth of record-keeping forms included in the appendices.

Romano, Tom. 2004. *Crafting authentic voice.* Portsmouth, NH: Heinemann.

Tom Romano has thirty years of experience writing and teaching writing. I find all his books to be that rare combination of sound theory and practical suggestions. *Crafting Authentic Voice* offers suggestions and rationale for teaching students to use their own voices in their writing. With inviting sidebars with "try this" strategies, readers have the bonus of working with infusing their own unique voices into all their writing. His examples include his own students' work as well as published authors. Highly recommended.

Classic (and Practical!) Texts by Major Researchers

It is very difficult to narrow down key resources by the leading theorists in the field. I chose these four texts because they marry theory and practice.

Calkins, Lucy. 1994. *The art of teaching writing.* Portsmouth, NH: Heinemann.

Lucy McCormack Calkins is a respected name in the field of writing instruction, and this text shows why. Though the length may be daunting, readers who want a complete "how-to" on the teaching of writing, with numerous examples and thoughtful rationale, will be grateful for this book. Her strategies and suggestions for writing conferences are particularly helpful.

Graves, Donald H. 2002. *Writing: Teachers and children at work.* Portsmouth, NH: Heinemann.

"Children want to write if we let them," Graves reminds us. His call for writing instruction in schools—a neglected content area in 1983—was embraced by grateful teachers and parents and the term *writing workshop* was coined. Donald Graves is widely acclaimed as the researcher who sparked the writing process movement in elementary schools. The twentieth anniversary edition of his classic text is a treat for a new generation of writing teachers at work with their students.

Murray, Donald M. 2004. *Write to learn,* 2nd ed. Portsmouth, NH: Heinemann.

Pulitzer prize–winning journalist and writing professor Donald Murray leads the reader through his own writing process. He builds theory from this exploration by adding his students' processes. The text works for both experienced and novice writers and teachers of writing. Donald Murray advocated teaching writing as a process at the college level, revolutionizing freshman composition across the country.

Routman, Regie. 2004. *Writing essentials: Raising expectations and results while simplifying teaching*. Portsmouth, NH: Heinemann.

Teachers love this resource book which is both research-based and eminently practical. The text is reader-friendly, though quite long. I find it a good text to refer to as a kind of resource guide rather than reading through each chapter chronologically. The DVD is an excellent companion that groups of teachers might watch together for follow-up discussion.

Readers Club Guide

1. **In most texts, oral language acquisition is a very separate topic from written language acquisition and development. Why do you think it is important to frame these two developmental processes highlighting the parallels?**

    There is a widespread understanding that learning to talk is developmental. Parents celebrate their babies' growing speaking abilities: we find approximations charming and know that this is a temporary stage; we talk back to babies babbling as if it makes sense to us, honoring that their words will come—and they do. On the other hand, there is a misconception that writing (and reading) somehow needs to be correct right from the start, and that teaching isolated skills in a rigid lockstep manner will lead to literacy. One of the key points I want to make in this book is that writing is also a process of *language acquisition and development*. As such, children need to be nurtured in similar ways, and through similar stages of growth.

2. **What is the benefit of parents, teachers, and caregivers understanding the developmental aspect of early literacy development?**

    Once teachers and caregivers can understand the parallels, they can begin to shift their stance to what they already know about young children's growing language abilities as they look at each child in the context of his or her literacy development. So much of the wonder of the human language is invisible to us; we take it for granted. What I love best about teaching language acquisition and development classes is that my students start reporting what they notice about the speech around them. They share with their families and with each other the marvels they overhear in conversation, patterns they notice in news reporting, and especially the brilliance of the young children in their daily lives. I want to promote that stance of wonder to the world of written language, so teachers, parents, and caregivers are as thrilled as I am when they notice the formation of a new convention a child has discovered, or the way they invent a new pattern in their spelling, or how they show passage of time brilliantly using a combination of words and pictures.

    And of course, a practical benefit for early childhood educators is that when they have a good grasp of the typical stages of development, they can support, nurture, and at times nudge when appropriate.

3. More schools are separating the focus in the curriculum into three very separate strands: oral language, reading, and writing. What do you see as the relationship among these language arts?

The term *language arts* is a very apt phrase to describe these related skills. And I would definitely include drawing as part of the language arts as well, a key component, not only for young children, but with all ages.

With very young children, though, it is especially misleading to look at these curricular components as isolated from each other. Most schools—even preschools—tend to focus on reading before writing, but as I document in the book, developmentally, children write before they read; they can *encode* language before they can *decode*. So we need to find ways to provide the tools to allow children to literally make their marks as a way to extend their literacy. I am heartened when I see teachers and parents littering the environment with pencils, markers, journals, pads of paper, chalkboards to provide that time to try out written language much as they have played with words and sounds in their speaking.

And reading-writing connections are also vital. Children get that important sense of story from being read to. This often sparks their interest in creating their own stories—and the pictures that are part of their writing. It all flows together.

4. What about the impact of new technologies on early writing development? Where does that fit in?

All writing is dependent on tools, whether it is the simple act of using a stick to write in the sand or the more sophisticated tools of computer technology. What I've noticed, and begun to document, is that the basic stages of literacy acquisition remain the same.

For example, my young friend Deanna, when she was only three, began to use her mother's computer in much the way she and other children begin to make their marks on the world through scribble writing. She just had more sophisticated tools in her environment. When she "wrote" to me on e-mail, she would "scribble" on the computer: she would type in letters, numbers, and symbols, then simply hit "send" as a way of passing what she had written to me. I'm delighted to see the many parallels between acquisition of computer writing and other writing young children do. It is not through specific instruction, but through providing access and more experienced learners, that young children acquire the ability to use the tools of computers as part of their literacy repertoire.

5. What is a current trend in the field of early literacy that is exciting to you?

I am very excited by the growth of genuine writing workshops in more and more preschools, kindergartens, and primary school classrooms. With more caregivers and family members welcomed into classrooms, they are seeing ways to build on the children's growing literacy skills. For example, in the Head Start classrooms I've observed here in Portland, Oregon, I'm seeing cutting-edge work with developing ways for young children to write their poems, their stories, their notes and observations of the world around them in a variety of ways. Best of all, these teachers recognize that "there is nothing as practical as a good theory" for understanding their young charges. They are using this deep understanding of young children's minds to create unique writing workshops specifically suited to their students.

6. What is a current trend that concerns you?

Well, there's the flip side, isn't there? Some early childhood programs are being pulled in a very different direction, toward more of a standardized "one-size fits-all" curriculum. The exploration, focus on creativity, and nurturing the whole child that were once the hallmarks of early childhood education are being pushed aside by top-down directives in the name of a more "academic" focus with children as young as three years old!

What were once standards for first graders have become benchmarks for entering kindergarten. I have seen three- and four-year-olds subjected to mind-numbing standardized tests that purport to measure their literacy in as little as sixty seconds. I am very troubled by this trend, though I see dedicated and knowledgeable educators and child advocates pushing back against these literacy directives and returning to a focus on the whole child.

7. What do you see as next important steps for researchers of early language and literacy to consider?

There needs to be a shift toward looking closely at *how* children acquire and use the tools of literacy. This means exploring their abilities in the real world of their literate cultures. It also means that researchers will need to be patient, listen closely, and look at the world of children through a new lens—one that respects children for their language-learning potential.

A decade ago, the world of oral language acquisition was radically changed by researchers beginning to frame questions that babies can answer. Long before they can speak, babies show their understanding through head-turning preference and other research models that are based on sustained observations of infants and toddlers as they acquire language. It's time to look at early writing attempts through the same vision of possibility.

This means interacting with young children as they are in the process of acquiring literacy in many different environments, from home to school to public places. It's really a very exciting time for literacy researchers!

8. **What is the best way to bring new research to communities of caregivers and teachers?**

The best way to my mind is to invite them to be partners in our research. Teachers and caregivers are experienced in reading the subtle cues and behaviors of the children with whom they spend their days. Once they see the importance of their observations, they are the perfect collaborators.

And beyond collaborating, teachers can form their own research communities at their schools, meeting to compare their observations, try out each others' ideas, and then share what they are learning with other schools and professional communities. It's the teacher-researcher model as professional development.

Many schools "jumpstart" their inquiry groups by having "reading book club" discussions around professional books. It is my hope that *Raising Writers* can serve to spark teacher-research groups that are interested in investigating early literacy acquisition and ways to nurture young writers.

Questions and Topics for Discussion

Note: These questions and suggested activities for exploring young children's writing assume that groups are reading _Raising Writers_ together and want to extend their reading by exploring the ideas in the book in more depth. The best way to investigate early writing development is by making connections between the theories and examples you've read, and your own investigations with the children you know and work with.

1. Looking at the continuum for language development, (Table 1.1, Chapter 1) choose one of the stages to investigate more closely for at least one week. Jot down anecdotal notes and collect actual samples of children's marks on a page. In small groups, share the data, noting where the stages overlap, as well as surprises and new questions that emerged as you investigated.

   At the end of your sharing, you might look ahead by describing what you will look at next in terms of development, and also how your work with the child or children might change based on what you have learned from this investigation.

2. One week prior to book group discussion, keep an anecdotal journal record of when a child surprised and "awed" you by her abilities. This simple strategy can help you be open to the daily wonder of children's abilities, and can provide a wonderful opening "ritual" for book group discussions.

3. The following four questions are reprinted from the end of Chapter 1:

   1. What is the history of this child and this piece of writing?

   2. What does this child show that she knows:

      a. About the world?

      b. About language?

   3. What is his intent in this piece of writing?

   4. How can I help her make her meaning clearer?

   Choose a child and one of his or her pieces of writing, then look at the piece of writing using these questions as a lens. The data that you share with your book group members will help guide you in continuing to approach writing using this stance.

4. To try out researching a very young child's written language, find a young child five years old or younger. If you are not currently working with young children, you might visit a Head Start program or a daycare setting. Ask the child to write you a story, and just observe what he or she writes. Ask the child to "read" the story back to you. What did you discover about what this child already knows about written language? With other members of your book group, compile a list of what the children know, and what tools you would want to provide the child to nurture his or her growth as a writer. It might also be interesting to note any patterns in gender differences.

5. Observe a child as he or she draws a picture or writes a story using pictures. Be sure to ask the child questions about what she is creating without making assumptions yourself. Bring your notes to share with your book group.

6. Keep track of the conventions that you notice children using in their writing for two weeks. Once you are focused on this aspect of their writing development, you'll most probably start seeing more than you had expected. The next step is to look for how the children are learning that convention from each other. What children seem to be informally teaching that question mark, action line, or exclamation point to others?

7. Having conferences with English language learners, especially those in the silent period, can be frustrating. Audio- or videotape yourself having a conference with an ELL child, then transcribe the tape. Bring your transcriptions to your inquiry group, discussing with your colleagues what you did well that you can build on, and what you might have done differently. As a group, you can acquire insights to help your conferences be more beneficial to the children with whom you work.

8. Since reading aloud to children is so vital to narrative growth and story sense, it can be very helpful to "talk books" with colleagues, especially those whom you find are working to capture the interest of young children. Plan a children's literature sharing night of "good reads." A wonderful extension is to share a compiled list with parents, inviting them to send back books that they have enjoyed with their children as well.

References

Anderson, Jeff. 2005. *Mechanically inclined.* Portland, ME: Stenhouse.

Applebee, Arthur. 1978. *The child's concept of story.* Chicago: University of Chicago Press.

Beers, J.W., & E. H. Henderson. 1977. A study of developing orthographic concepts among first graders. *Research in the Teaching of English, 11,* 133–148.

Bell, Sylvia, & Mary Ainsworth. 1972. Infant crying and maternal responsiveness. *Child Development, 43,* 1171–1190.

Bissex, Glenda. 1980. *GNYS AT WRK: A child learns to read and write.* Cambridge, MA: Harvard University Press.

Bloom, L. 1993. *The transition from infancy to language.* Cambridge, UK: Cambridge University Press.

Bridge, Susan. 1988. Squeezing from the middle of the tube. In N. Atwell & T. Newkirk (Eds.), *Understanding writing: Ways of observing, learning, and teaching K–8* (2nd ed., pp. 80–87). Portsmouth, NH: Heinemann.

Bruner, Jerome. 1983. *Child's talk: Learning to use language.* New York: W. W. Norton.

Calkins, Lucy. 1980. When children want to punctuate: Basic skills belong in context. *Language Arts, 57,* 567–573.

Chi, M. 1988. Invented spelling/writing in Chinese-speaking children: The developmental patterns. In J. Readance & R. Baldwin (Eds.), *Dialogue in literacy research* (37th Yearbook, National Reading Conference, pp. 285–296). Chicago: National Reading Conference.

Chomsky, Carol. (1971). Invented spelling in an open classroom. *Word, 27,* 499–518.

Dyson, Anne Haas. 1988. Appreciate the drawing and dictating of young children. *Young Children, 43* (3), 25–32.

Dyson, Anne Haas. 2003. *The brothers and sisters learn to write: Popular literacies in childhood and school cultures.* New York: Teachers College Press.

Dyson, Anne Haas. 2004. Literacy "basics" in childhood spaces: A critical perspective on the "basics." In Y. Goodman (Ed.), *Critical issues in early literacy development.* Portsmouth, NH: Heinemann.

Edelsky, Carole. 1982. Writing in a bilingual program: The relation of L1 and L2 texts. *TESOL Quarterly, 16,* 211–228.

Edelsky, Carole. 1983. Segmentation and punctuation: Developmental data from young writers in a bilingual program. *Research in the Teaching of English, 17,* 135–136.

Edelsky, Carole, & Katharine Jilbert. 1985. Bilingual children and writing: A lesson for us all. *Volta Review, 87* (5), 57–72.

Ernst, G., & K. J. Richard. 1995. Reading and writing pathways to conversation in the ESL classroom. *The Reading Teacher 48,* 320–326.

Ernst, Karen. 1992. *Picturing learning.* Portsmouth, NH: Heinemann.

Ferreiro, Emilia. 1980. The relationship between oral and written language: The children's viewpoints. In M. Haussler, D. Strickland, & Y. Goodman (Eds.), *Oral and written language development research: Impact on the schools,* (pp. 47–56). Urbana, IL: International Reading Association.

Ferreiro, Emilia, & Ana Teberosky. 1982. *Literacy before schooling.* Portsmouth, NH: Heinemann.

Freeman, Yvonne, & David Freeman. 2003. *Between worlds.* Portsmouth, NH: Heinemann.

Gerritz, K. E. 1974. First graders' spelling of vowels: An exploratory study. Doctoral Dissertation, Harvard Graduate School of Education.

Gibson, J. 1966. *The senses considered as perceptual system.* Boston: Houghton Mifflin.

Gibson, J., & P. Yonas. 1968. A new theory of scribbling and drawing in children. In H. Levin, E. J. Gibson, & J. J. Gibson (Eds.), *The analysis of reading skill* (Final Report). Washington, DC: U.S. Department of Health, Education, and Welfare, Office of Education.

Golinkoff, Roberta, & Kathy Hirsh-Pasek. 2000. *How babies talk.* New York: Penguin Books.

Graves, Donald. 2002. *Writing: Teachers and children at work.* Portsmouth, NH: Heinemann.

Graves, Donald, & Virginia Stuart. 1985. *Write from the start: Tapping your child's natural writing ability.* New York: E. P. Dutton.

Harste, Jerome, Virginia Woodward, & Carolyn Burke. 1984. *Language stories and literacy lessons.* Portsmouth, NH: Heinemann.

Hart, B., & T. Risley. 1995. *Meaningful differences in the everyday experiences of young American children.* Baltimore: Brooks.

Heath, Shirley Brice. 1982. *Ways with words.* Cambridge, UK: Cambridge University Press.

Hilliker, Judy. 1988. Labeling to beginning narrative: Four kindergarten children learn to write. In N. Atwell & T. Newkirk (Eds.), *Understanding writing: Ways of observing, learning, and teaching K–8* (2nd ed., pp. 14–22). Portsmouth, NH: Heinemann.

Hubbard, Ruth. 1985. Write and tell. *Language Arts, 62* (6), 624–630.

Hubbard, Ruth. 1989. *Authors of pictures, draughtsmen of words.* Portsmouth, NH: Heinemann.

Huddleson, Sarah. 1989. A tale of two children. In D. M. Johnson & D. H. Roen (Eds.), *Richness in writing* (pp. 84–99). New York: Longman.

Hughes, Margaret, & Dennis Searle. 1997. *The violent E and other tricky sounds: Learning to spell in kindergarten through grade 6.* Portland, ME: Stenhouse.

Krashen, Stephen. 1985. *The input hypothesis: Issues and implications.* London: Longman.

Leondar, Bruce. 1977. Hatching plots: Genesis of storymaking. In D. Perkins and B. Leondar (Eds.), *The arts and cognition* (pp. 172–191). Baltimore: Johns Hopkins University Press.

Lionni, Leo. 1984. Before images. *The Horn Book*, 726–734.

Miller, P., & J. J. Goodnow. 1995. Cultural practices: Toward an integration of culture and development. In J. J. Goodnow, P. J. Miller, & F. Kessel (Eds.), *Cultural practices as contexts for development, No. 67, New directions in child development* (pp. 5–16). San Francisco: Jossey-Bass.

Petito, L. A., & P. F. Marentette. 1991. Babbling in the manual mode: Evidence for the ontogeny of language. *Science, 251,* 1493–1496.

Ray, Katie Wood, & Lisa Cleaveland. 2006. *Study driven: A framework for planning units of study in the writing workshop.* Portsmouth, NH: Heinemann.

Read, Charles. 1971. Pre-school children's knowledge of English phonology. *Harvard Educational Review, 41,* 1–34.

Rogoff, B. 1990. *Apprenticeship in thinking: Cognitive development in social context.* New York: Oxford University Press.

Sachs, J., B. Bard, & M. S. Johnson. 1981. Language learning with restricted input: Case studies of two hearing children of deaf parents. *Applied Psycholinguistics, 2,* 33–54.

Samway, Katharine Davies. 2006. *When English language learners write.* Portsmouth, NH: Heinemann.

Schecter, S., & R. Bayley. 2002. *Languge as cultural practice: Mexicanos en el Norte.* Mahwah, NJ: Lawrence Erlbaum.

Schiefflin, Bambi, & Elinor Ochs. 1983. A cultural perspective on the transition from prelinguistic to linguistic communication. In R. M. Golinkoff (Ed.), *The transition from prelinguistic to linguistic communication* (pp. 115–31). Hillsdale, NJ: Lawrence Erlbaum.

Smith, Frank. 2003. *Unspeakable acts, unnatural practices: Flaws and fallacies in "scientific reading" instruction.* Portsmouth, NH: Heinemann.

Stern, Daniel. 1990. *Diary of a baby.* New York: Basic Books.

Taylor, Denny. 2000. Facing hardships: Jamestown and colonial life. In K. D. Samway (Ed.), *Integrating the ESL standards into classroom practice: Grades 3–5* (pp. 53–81). Alexandria, VA: Teachers of English to Speakers of Other Languages.

Vygotsky, L. V. 1986. *Thought and language.* Cambridge, MA: MIT Press.

Watson-Gageo, Karen. 1992. Thick explanation in the ethnographic study of child socialization. In W. Corsaro & P. J. Miller (Eds.), *Interpretive approaches to children's socialization, No. 58, New directions for child development* (pp. 51–66). San Francisco: Jossey-Bass.

Wells, Gordon. 1986. *The meaning makers: Children learning language and using language to learn.* Portsmouth, NH: Heinemann.

Wilde, Sandra. 1993. *You kan red this!: Spelling and punctuation for whole language classrooms.* Portsmouth, NH: Heinemann.

Index